**Protecting Your Homestead**
*Using a rifle to defend life on your property*

**By Grant Cunningham**

Copyright 2018, Grant Cunningham and Personal Security Institute LLC. All rights reserved.

Published by Personal Security Institute LLC.

The information in this book is meant to supplement, not replace, proper self defense training. Like any physical activity, self defense training poses some inherent risk. The author and publisher advise readers to take full responsibility for their safety and know their limits. Before practicing the skills described in this book, be sure that your equipment is well maintained, and do not take risks beyond your level of experience, aptitude, training, and comfort level.

Although the author and publisher have made every effort to ensure that the information in this book was correct at press time, the author and publisher do not assume and hereby disclaim any liability to any party for any loss, damage, or disruption caused by errors or omissions, whether such errors or omissions result from negligence, accident, or any other cause.

# FREE BOOK OFFER!

I've written a book on choosing defensive ammunition that will help you pick the right ammo for your handgun, rifle, or shotgun. It explains how ammunition works in simple terms and what you should look for at your local gun store.

You can get your FREE copy of *How To Choose Self Defense Ammunition* just by clicking or going to this link on my site:

www.getgrant.us/PYH

# CONTENTS

| | |
|---|---|
| Acknowledgments | vii |
| Introduction | ix |
| 1. Safety First! | 1 |
| 2. What Is Perimeter Defense? | 5 |
| 3. Ethical and Legal Considerations | 11 |
| 4. Context and Expectations | 19 |
| 5. Rifles for Perimeter Defense | 25 |
| 6. Sighting Options | 39 |
| 7. The Utility Rifle | 53 |
| 8. Accessories | 61 |
| 9. Ammunition | 73 |
| 10. Storing and Retrieving Your Rifle | 85 |
| 11. Handling the Rifle | 99 |
| 12. Zeroing the Rifle | 119 |
| 13. Accuracy, Precision, and Time | 131 |
| 14. Aiming Concepts | 143 |
| 15. Trigger Control | 151 |
| 16. Shooting Positions | 159 |
| 17. Moving to the Threat | 179 |
| 18. Shouldering and Firing | 191 |
| 19. Training and Practicing Perimeter Defense | 197 |
| 20. Parting Thoughts | 203 |
| Facebook discussion group | 207 |
| Also by Grant Cunningham | 209 |
| About the Author | 211 |

# ACKNOWLEDGMENTS

I have the privilege of knowing and working with a number of amazing people who have helped me put this book together. Without them, you wouldn't be reading this now!

Special thanks go to my Launch Team, who helped me review and polish the material you're about to read:

Mike Iñigo, John Hintermaier, John Flynn, George Prudden, John R. Dinkel, Zachary Murphy, Mark Chudzicki, Michael A. Kelly, chris myers, Randy Giedrycz, Dr. David F. Simpson, Kevin H. Mowry, Dr. Greg Hutchens, Mike Boyle, James Nyffeler, Scott Reisenauer, Robert T. Hodges, Dave Carlson, Patrick S. Coons, Steve Antoine, Thomas C. Stuart, Ben Walton, Douglas Nelson, and Ken Jennings.

My friends Joshua Gideon and Julie & Andy Loeffler have shown me both unwavering support and uncensored opinion. I thank them for always being honest even when I didn't want to hear it.

If you think great writers are born, they're not — they're the product of great editors! My editor, who takes the raw manuscript and turns it into something worth reading, is Kathy Allard.

My wife Chris, to whom I've been married for over thirty years, gets the most credit for serving as my sounding board, cheerleader, and occasional photographer and model. Were it not for her, this wouldn't have even gotten started (which is standard operating procedure in our house).

Finally, thanks to YOU for supporting my work!

— Grant Cunningham

March 2018

# INTRODUCTION

This book has been rather easy to write and, at the same time, quite hard to explain!

In the last decade or so, the idea of the defensive rifle has been sold as a replacement for, and a more powerful version of, the handgun. Its use as a home-defense tool inside the home has come to be what most people think of when the subject is raised.

Don't get me wrong — there is a place for that application in what is usually termed "close-quarters battle" (CQB), which is what defense inside the home is. With most people living in urban or close suburban environs, it's not surprising that CQB rifle techniques have taken center stage.

But when you consider defense outside of the typical 50x100 foot lot of suburbia, the situation changes. Self-defense in the country or on a homestead is different than it is in the suburbs. You have to worry about threats to your family and your livestock, and the potential attackers include two- and four-legged predators.

The distances are also greater. Instead of dealing with an intruder across the room, you might be dealing with a predator across the yard

— or across the field. Most importantly, instead of you being the victim (or being in close proximity to the victim), the life you're protecting might be a lot closer to its attacker than to you.

This is where the defensive rifle comes into its own. The rifle is the tool to use when you need precision and power at distance. This kind of defense — which I call "perimeter defense," or protecting lives out to the limits of your property line — is the subject of this book.

Unlike most books written about the defensive rifle, *Protecting Your Homestead* looks at how to use a rifle beyond what is generally considered handgun range. Instead of teaching you how to use the rifle inside the home, this book shows you how to use it the way a rifle was designed to be used — quickly, accurately, and at extended distance.

In this book, you'll learn how to pick the right rifle for the job of perimeter defense; the best and most flexible calibers; how to zero your rifle (and why it's important); choosing and using sights and optics; shooting positions from fastest to most stable; how to properly store, retrieve, and move to the threat with your rifle; how to get to your first shot quickly and accurately; and much more.

If you live in the country, or plan to, this is the defensive rifle information you need to know. Let's get started!

## Chapter One
# SAFETY FIRST!

Like many other items in your home, firearms are very useful tools when handled properly, but quickly become dangerous when mishandled. Whenever you're handling your perimeter defense rifle, or any firearm, it's important that you follow some simple rules to keep everyone safe.

### Safety rules

Rules are universal behavioral guidelines: They are always applicable and should never be violated. While some specific or situational procedures might be required by the range you're using, you should always observe three universal rules whenever you're handling any firearm.

*1. Always keep the muzzle pointed in a generally safe direction.*

What is a generally safe direction? One in which, should the gun fire, you will not injure anyone. On a shooting range, the berm or bullet trap behind the target is a generally safe direction, and depending on the surface, the ground may be as well. There may be other generally safe directions that are location specific. Of course other shooters, staff, onlookers, and your own body parts are never a generally safe direction!

**2. Always keep your trigger finger outside of the trigger guard unless you're actually shooting.**

The preferred place is on the frame above the trigger. In the case of the rifle, it means the frame space or stock area above the trigger. The exact position may vary due to rifle design, but it does not mean resting on the trigger guard itself!

**3. Always remember that you are in control of an object that, if used recklessly or negligently, can injure or kill.**

This rule is at the heart of all the other safety rules. It means to always think about what you're doing with your firearm. It encompasses all those other safety rules you might see on posters and signs at the range: making sure of your target, making sure you know where the bullets will land, using the right ammunition for the gun, keeping your gun out of the hands of unauthorized users, etc. It should instill in your mind an ***attitude*** about safety without providing an endless checklist of items to remember.

*Safety procedures*

Rules are universally applicable, while procedures are situational and help you implement the rules and keep yourself and other people safe. Procedures tend to be range- or activity-specific, and you may find some of them listed at your range.

## Safe storage

While I hate to repeat myself, I'm going to remind you about that third rule: *Always remember that you are in control of an object that, if used recklessly or negligently, can injure or kill.* As I explained, this is the rule that instills in your mind an attitude about safety and encompasses all those "other" rules you see on posters at shooting ranges.

One of the rules you might see on such a poster is to keep your gun locked up so others can't accidentally harm themselves or others. As a responsible gun owner, it's your job to keep your guns out of the reach of people who shouldn't have access to them and people you haven't authorized to have access. This responsibility goes hand in hand with the right to keep and bear arms, and it's one that unfortunately too few gun owners understand until it's too late.

It's easy to find news stories where a child has been injured or killed because they found a gun and played with it. In almost every case, it's because the gun wasn't properly secured — and those cases are all preventable.

*In your hands or locked up*

My general rule is that there are only two proper places for a firearm: on your person (or otherwise within your immediate control) or securely locked away. While Second Amendment purists lambast me for saying that, I believe it's the best rule for the responsible gun owner to follow.

The usual response I get is, "If it's locked up, it's no good for self-defense!" That may have been true in the 1960s, but in the 21st century we have storage devices that not only make it easy to access a defensive handgun when needed, but also to keep unauthorized people from gaining easy access*. We'll cover the options in more depth in the chapter on Retrieval.

*Unsafe storage: hiding guns*

The worst option is just hiding or stashing guns around the house. Many people put their guns on a high shelf or cabinet in the mistaken belief their children can't climb that high, or an intruder would never look there. Neither is true!

Small children have an amazing ability to reach even the most inconveniently stored guns. Never underestimate the ability of a child to climb. Also don't underestimate their curiosity or observational skills. If you have a gun, no matter how careful you are to hide it from them, they probably know you have it and likely know where it is. After that, it's just a matter of figuring out how to get to it — and children often do, with tragic results.

Criminals, too, know where people — including you — are likely to hide firearms. It might slow down their search a bit, but if they suspect firearms are in the house, they're very likely to go looking for them. If they do, they'll likely find them. The best way to keep your guns "off the street" is to lock them up.

Secure your perimeter defense rifle —don't just hide it.

—

*\* - Nothing is perfect, and there is no completely infallible method to keep determined people away from your guns. Understand that any security device can be defeated, but that's no excuse not to use them.*

*Chapter Two*

## WHAT IS PERIMETER DEFENSE?

Since the turn of this century, perhaps a bit longer, it's been fashionable to teach the use of the defensive rifle as a substitute for the handgun. Techniques to use the rifle in "close quarters battle" (CQB) have been promoted by an almost endless number of firearms trainers — many of them veterans of our various wars in the Middle East, where the use of the rifle in urban warfare has been developed to a very high degree.

When those techniques are applied to civilian (self-defense) use, they almost invariably center on the rifle's use inside the home against an intruder or intruders. Movement inside the structure, with rifle in hand and a flashlight attached, is a common feature. Shooting distances tend to stay inside the longest expected indoor shot, and I've seen more than one such class where shots beyond 25 feet or so simply weren't taught.

There is value in knowing how to use your rifle for defense inside your home, and I encourage you to take advantage of those resources to learn the specifics. What's missing from much of the current defensive rifle doctrine, though, is the concept of defending yourself outside the confines of your house.

For those who live anywhere beyond suburbia, where it's plausible to face a threat at distances greater than across your living room, such courses fall short of a comprehensive skill set. If you live on acreage or out in the country, you may need to defend yourself beyond the walls of your house — out to your perimeter.

## The nature of perimeter defense

Perimeter defense was born from the needs of those who live in an environment where properties are larger than a typical 50x100-foot suburban lot. In areas where properties are measured in acres instead of square feet, the risks faced by residents are different and so are their defensive needs.

In such environments, it's not uncommon to face both animal and human predators, and while the rules of engagement differ, they have something in common: They usually present themselves as a threat at longer ranges than the typical suburban home.

That's why I define perimeter defense as the use of a firearm — specifically a rifle — against an identified threat beyond what is normally considered handgun range. Perimeter defense means protecting yourself, your family, and your livestock against predators at any reasonable and justifiable distance, out to the limits of your property line.

### *Threats change in the country*

The suburbanite usually thinks of threats solely in terms of human adversaries, which is appropriate for that environment. But in a more rural setting, humans aren't the only threat — predatory animals are often a danger to people and livestock.

A coyote attacking a calf, for instance, is most definitely a threat requiring rapid intervention at a distance. Feral dogs, particularly those roaming in packs, are a common issue for owners of livestock, and have been known to attack humans as well. Rabid animals are a risk to everyone and everything, while less dangerous pests such as skunks are best dealt with at much greater than arm's length!

This isn't to imply that human threats don't exist in the country, because they most assuredly do. Home invasions happen in the country just as they do closer to town, as do personal and sexual assaults. It's tempting to think of country living as being free from crime worries, but that's not at all the case. Crime happens less frequently simply due to lower population density, but it does happen. Longer distances between houses means neighbors are less intrusive, but it also means you're out of sight and earshot of people who can come to your aid, which makes criminal attacks somewhat less risky for the perpetrators.

At the same time, having a house that's set off the road by some distance means a longer early warning period and more opportunity to intercede before an attack actually happens. It's not uncommon to identify and deter a potential threat well before he gets into the "average" range for self-defense shootings. Those longer distances also mean that if someone displays criminal intent, the problem may begin some distance away and necessitate a tool with greater range than the handgun can easily deliver.

That tool is the rifle.

**Advantage: Rifle**

The rifle has three major advantages over the handgun. First, it can deliver much greater precision than the handgun. With four points of contact with the body instead of one\*, the rifle is more stable. More stability means greater achievable precision. The sight radius of the rifle is also much greater than that of the handgun, further increasing potential precision.

Second, the rifle has more raw power than the typical handgun. Depending on the calibers of comparison, the rifle often delivers more power at 100 yards than the handgun will at the muzzle. The rifle easily penetrates intervening obstacles, like car doors, that can (depending on exactly where they're hit) deflect or even stop pistol bullets.

Third, the combination of greater precision and more power means the rifle can reliably deliver overwhelming force at a much greater distance than the average handgun (even when the latter is wielded by an above-average shooter).

Rifles also have the advantage of easily attached magnifying optical sights (scopes), which not only enhance precision but also make it easier to see and verify the threat before the trigger is pressed.

All of this makes the rifle the preferred tool when distances are measured in yards rather than feet, when targets are crouched or low to the ground, when vision is obscured by rain or dusk, or when targets are moving. The rifle is the tool to separate the predator from the flock, to handle multiple members of a pack, or to demonstrate resolve to the belligerent interloper.

*Using the rifle responsibly*

But this enhanced capability has a downside. The lack of ready witnesses and nosy neighbors in a rural setting can make it easy, perhaps too easy, to employ the rifle in situations that do not warrant the use of lethal force. Intimidating someone with a rifle when they've displayed no articulable threat (or potential threat) can become a legal problem should the offended party summon law enforcement.

Pulling the trigger is an act that should always be done deliberately and with full cognizance of the potential ramifications. Shooting at someone's pet simply because they crossed a fenceline, for instance, has more than once resulted in arrests and lawsuits. I'll have more to say about this in a later chapter, but using the rifle in the country requires the same discretion as the handgun in the city.

**My story**

I grew up on a farm where the rifle (and, to a lesser extent, the shotgun) was a common tool. It was used to put down sick cattle, protect calves from predators, and on occasion deter someone who saw the farm as easy pickings for crime. Because we had attractive hunting and fishing grounds on our property, armed trespassers were not uncommon — and law enforcement was a considerable distance away during the days before cell phones and the 9-1-1 system had been invented. We were, in the truest sense, on our own, and I learned to deal with all of these situations at a very early age.

After going to college and spending some time living in suburbia, my wife and I returned to the country. The countryside is definitely less bucolic than it was when I was a kid, with clandestine drug labs and associated violence becoming more common. In addition, encroaching development has affected wildlife patterns and predators are more common than I remember them being.

I find myself using the rifle more often than my father did, and firing more rounds in defense of my family and livestock than he ever shot. While almost all my defensive rifle use has been against animals, I've had more than one human encounter that required the rifle to defuse.

At the same time, I'm a self-defense and preparedness educator, and in that role I've taken (and taught) many "urban rifle"-type courses. A critical examination of those courses, filtered through my personal knowledge and experience using the rifle as a defensive tool, led me to identify their weaknesses and make substantive changes to fit my own environment. This book, and my Perimeter Defense rifle course on which it is based, are the result of my desire to bring realistic and relevant rifle skills to the people who really need them.

## About this book

In the following pages, you'll find my personal approach to the defensive rifle in the context of defense outside the footprint of your house. This is not a book about patrolling your property, nor does it contain information on clearing structures with your rifle. Instead, you'll find information about using the rifle as a defensive tool beyond what you normally think of as handgun distances — say, 50 feet or so to about 100 yards (perhaps a bit more), which is the practical limit for most people on most property against most threats.

The rifle is the defensive tool that must be retrieved from storage and transported to the point of use. Because of that defining characteristic, you'll find information on handling and movement specific to those tasks. We'll also cover safe handling, shooting positions applicable to defensive rifle shooting, how to shoot quickly and accurately without staging or choreographing your movements, and how to choose the best hardware and ammunition for the job of perimeter defense.

If you've had some training in "urban rifle" courses, or perhaps military or law enforcement experience, some of my recommendations may seem to border on heresy! If you read something that doesn't sit well with your existing knowledge, I urge you to do two things: First, consider the context of use (defense of self, family, and homestead). Second, pay attention to the explanations given. I've found that, in most cases, once the reason for the technique (or hardware) recommendation is understood, the disagreement disappears.

In other words, I have very specific reasons for what I recommend and what I teach and advocate — and I'll do my very best to explain them in ways that make sense to you and your life!

---

\* - *Even using two hands, the handgun still only has one effective point of contact with the body because the hands are overlapped.*

## Chapter Three
# ETHICAL AND LEGAL CONSIDERATIONS

**Preface:** *I am not a lawyer, and what follows is not legal advice. You should contact a lawyer versed in the laws of self-defense and defense of others for an opinion on the statutes in your area.*

I review a lot of shooting incidents as part of evaluating what does and doesn't work in self-defense. When I look at defensive gun uses where the incident did not turn out to the defender's benefit, the failure is rarely due to a lack of shooting skill. Most of the failures are due to improperly identifying the target or, worse yet, incorrectly judging if lethal force was even warranted.

Understanding the myriad areas where the use of lethal force (your firearm) is and is not appropriate or justifiable is beyond the scope of this book. In fact, whole books have been written about the subject. I strongly urge you to take a class on the use of deadly force, or at least obtain, read, and frequently re-read a good book on the subject. The best source I know for such information is Massad Ayoob, and his book and course are highly recommended.*

**The negative outcome**

There is something we don't often talk about in the world of defensive training, but it's incredibly important to understand. In any encounter, particularly with other human beings, there is a greater-than-zero chance of it ending badly for you in some way. We call this a negative outcome.**

In other words, anytime you do anything in self-defense — from yelling at someone to get off your driveway, to investigating the "bump in the night," to pointing a firearm at an attacker — there is a chance it will not turn out the way you intended. That chance is larger than most people believe, and it occurs with some regularity.

I could regale you for pages recounting such incidents. From the man who confronted a shoplifter and got stabbed for his effort to the fellow who shot at what he believed to be someone stealing his car only to find out he just killed his son, negative outcomes abound.

*The impact on your life*

Even when the outcome isn't physically injurious, it can still be quite negative. One of my fellow defensive shooting instructors intervened in a domestic incident where a man was viciously beating his wife in public. He drew his legally carried handgun, put himself between the man and woman, and ordered the man to the ground. The man complied, no shots were fired, and the police arrived and arrested the wife-beater. The local papers labeled him a hero.

Sounds good, doesn't it? It didn't really work out that way. He had to take time off work to appear at the various interviews, hearings, and depositions that come with being a witness in a felony assault case. Naturally he also had to make time to testify at the criminal trial. He used up all his vacation time and had to take unpaid time off from work.

This all contributed to him losing his comfortable white-collar job. It also made it very difficult to find another job. Not only were his prospective employers expected to accommodate the justice system's often capricious schedule, there was also a publicity problem — namely, the companies he interviewed with said they "didn't want the publicity" that went with his name (I'm sure they meant the notoriety of employing a man known to carry a firearm, but the result is the same).

Did I mention this happened in "gun friendly" Texas? No matter where you live, the possibility of an unforeseen negative outcome exists.

I don't intend this discussion to scare you into submission, to cause you to hide under your sheets and do nothing. Quite the contrary! I just want you to understand that the good guy doesn't always get the girl and ride off into the sunset, and to use the knowledge of that reality to make better decisions.

For example, using lethal force (or even the threat of lethal force) against another human being to prevent a property theft is rarely a good decision. You have insurance for a reason. The value of that property isn't worth taking another human's life, and it's definitely not worth risking yours.

If you are killed (or permanently disabled) trying to keep someone from taking your pickup truck, who sees to the needs of your family? The same question goes if you kill a 16-year-old joyrider and end up in prison because there was no threat to your life. All in all, it's better to call the police and let them recover it.

Be very clear: I'm not siding with criminals when I say this. I'm siding with you and your safety, and with your family, who need you alive, in one piece, and unencumbered. Be smart; make good decisions and avoid the negative outcome.

## Unique challenges of perimeter defense

When we think of the use of lethal force in defense, whether it be to protect ourselves or a loved one, we usually think in terms of our (the defender's) distance to the threat — the assumption being that the defender and the victim are either the same person, or they're in close proximity to each other.

Most use-of-force decisions are made on that assumption, focusing on the distance between the attacker and the defender. Generally speaking, the closer the defender is to the danger posed by the attacker, the more justifiable the defender is in his or her use of force.

Let's take a very simplified (and wholly unrealistic) example: A man armed with a knife is 10 feet in front of you and acting in a manner that leads you to believe he's intent on rushing you and stabbing you to death. That's a pretty clear-cut*** instance where your use of a defensive firearm is articulable and likely to be legally defensible.

Now, let's say that same knife-wielding maniac is the ex-husband of a woman you know, and she's standing in proximity to you. This is a case where the attacker is intent on harming another innocent person. Your use of your firearm to protect her life is an example of defense of another innocent person, and again may be justifiable — if the man were truly acting in a manner that would lead a reasonable person to conclude he was in fact intent on murdering the woman.

In perimeter defense, though, we often face a different scenario: The attacker, the victim, and the defender may be three different parties, and the space between the attacker and victim is likely to be much closer than that of the attacker and defender.

In this case, I can give you a realistic example: Your wife rushes into the room to tell you that your new calf is being chased by a coyote. You grab your rifle and head for the door. When you get onto your deck, you can clearly see the calf being chased by the coyote, and they're about 70 yards away from you.

The distance from you (the defender) to the attacker (the coyote) isn't the issue. It's the distance from the attacker to the victim (the calf) that establishes the danger. In this scenario, that distance may be a few feet — or maybe just inches.

In the world of defensive shooting, we train extensively for the scenario where shoot/no shoot decisions are based on our distance to the threat. In perimeter defense, your decision to use lethal force may instead be based on the distance of the attacker to a victim that is not you, nor in close proximity to you.

This is the kind of scenario that, while not unique to perimeter defense, plays a large part in defining the techniques and equipment used for the task. You may be facing an attacker that isn't necessarily focused on you and may not be in close proximity to you — but still poses an immediate threat. That isn't usually the case in suburbia!

*The attacking pet*

The example with the coyote is an easy decision. What if it were someone's pet dog, and it was stalking but not yet attacking the calf? Pets are a different class of animal, and blithely shooting a dog that belongs to someone is often prosecuted under cruelty to animals statutes. Exceptions are almost always made for dogs that attack humans, and many rural areas have statutes that excuse the killing of pets when they attack livestock.

The neighbor's dog that attacks and is in the process of killing your chickens, for instance, might fall into that exception.**** Even though you may be a distance from the threat, the fact that the attacker is in close proximity to his victim(s) is what necessitates and justifies your defensive use of lethal force. At the same time, people are often irrational about their pets — and the justice system, being made of people, is often irrational as well where dogs are concerned.

I've encountered cases where people have killed dogs in seemingly complete justification but were later charged. Some of those cases involved a neighbor's dog attacking another dog, the owner of the victimized dog having killed the attacking dog. Such events don't seem to be covered under livestock predation statutes (pets not being considered livestock), nor was a human life in danger, so the shooter was prosecuted. This is a grey area that seems to be dependent on the prosecutor and mood of the courts in the jurisdiction.

If you live in an unincorporated area where livestock protection laws are in force, this may not be a problem. You do, however, need to be sure what your local laws define as "livestock"; sometimes that definition applies only to cattle and horses, and not to sheep, goats, or chickens. As I've pointed out, they are unlikely to apply to your dogs.

As mentioned, the use of lethal force against a dog attacking a human being is generally tolerated in most jurisdictions. But it's important to note that shooting a dog that is merely aggressive and has not made physical contact may or may not be seen favorably by the law in your area. Judging by the cases I've seen, it usually isn't.

Again: It's worth speaking with a local defense attorney who can guide you in both the law and the mood of the court in your area. Shooting someone else's dog is always going to be an uncertain course of action even if you believe it to be fully justified.

Unless you are in actual, immediate danger of being mauled by a dog, I suggest trying other options — throwing rocks, yelling, calling Animal Control — before resorting to your rifle. The legal and social quagmire of shooting someone's pet is just that deep.

*The dog pack*

A scourge in many rural areas caused by the dumping of unwanted pets is the feral dog pack. Dogs are social animals and, left to their own devices, rarely choose to live a solitary life. They gather into packs and hunt, and sometimes that hunt involves the livestock on area farms.

If you have smaller livestock or newborn animals, the feral pack may be a serious threat. The cautions about shooting pets may not always apply to the dog pack, which is often seen (particularly in ranching areas) as a group of wild animals rather than someone's feisty fido. At the risk of repeating myself, contact a lawyer in your area who is familiar with this topic for guidance — and understand that the justice system isn't always consistent in such matters.

Your use of lethal force always brings with it the risk of prosecution or civil action. There is no absolute, you're-always-covered-if-you-do-this-one-thing answer. This is why it's so important for you to understand not just the law, but how it's applied in your area, and temper that with the reality that your decision to shoot can always be second-guessed.

---

\* - *I strongly recommend Mas Ayoob's book, "Deadly Force", and his course "MAG-20 Classroom" as the best introductions to the judicious use of deadly force available:*

*https://massadayoobgroup.com/mag-20-classroom/*

\*\* - *The term comes from colleague Claude Werner, "The Tactical Professor," who delves into this topic much more deeply on his blog. https://tacticalprofessor.wordpress.com*

\*\*\* - *Clear-cut but unlikely; attackers with knives don't usually alert you of their intentions in a way that gives you an opportunity to mount an efficient defense. Subterfuge and misdirection are more likely.*

\*\*\*\* - *I've observed that shooting someone else's pet, even when legally defensible, almost always results in civil proceedings — a surprisingly large percentage of which are successful for the litigant. Shooting someone's dog is a risky proposition even if it's not a crime under certain conditions.*

## Chapter Four
# CONTEXT AND EXPECTATIONS

In this book, you'll come across the words "context" and "plausibility." They're important concepts when applied to defensive shooting.

**Context**

One of the most important ideas in all of defensive training is context. Context means the environment in which something can be used or understood. Everything has a context in which it makes sense and in which it's usable, including defensive shooting skills, techniques, and ideas.

This book looks at private-sector self-defense on a homestead — you protecting your own life, the lives of your loved ones, your pets, and your livestock — against two- or four-legged predators. This is in contrast to a military context, a law enforcement context, or a competition shooting context, where the rules of engagement, the circumstances under which force is used, and the skills and techniques are different. What is appropriate for or important to a soldier or a cop or a competitive shooter is often very different than what's important to you and your family.

Of course some overlap exists among those contexts, because much of the actual physical shooting part of each job is similar. In other words, controlling a trigger is pretty much the same whether you're dealing with an attacking coyote or an enemy soldier. Some technique is in fact interchangeable.

But knowing how to evaluate any technique or piece of equipment for its application in your context is important to being able to spot when something isn't applicable to the job you need to do. You make that evaluation by understanding the context where something makes sense, and how that context is different than yours.

Context is a very useful tool to help evaluate techniques and ideas. Everything you'll learn in this book is based on the context of the worst-case scenario for the citizen defender: the attack you didn't anticipate occurring, to which you must mount a defense, and where shooting is the correct response.

That is the context of perimeter defense, and everything you're going to learn is optimized for that task.

**Is it plausible?**

Many things in this world are possible, in the sense that the laws of physics do not preclude them from occurring. But that doesn't mean everything is equally likely to occur! Many, perhaps most, of the things that are possible are exceedingly unlikely to happen. Life has a huge range of possibilities, some of which could happen, and many more that won't. It's useful to think of it this way: Everything that could happen is possible, but not everything that's possible could really happen!

This leaves us with something of a dilemma. As we prepare and equip ourselves to face a range of threats there will be some that are far more likely to happen, and some which might be possible but which we know aren't going to occur.

I've used this example in my classes for years (and only recently discovered it was the plot of a popular movie):* North Korean paratroopers take over a shopping mall. It's certainly possible, in the sense that the laws of physics do not prevent North Koreans from being paratroopers, but I think you can agree it's not at all likely. In fact, it is for all intents and purposes a fantasy scenario.

Let's say, though, that you didn't differentiate between likely and possible in your planning and spent your time preparing and training for the arrival of those enemy paratroopers. That's time, energy, and money that couldn't be used to prepare for the far more likely event of, say, an attempted homestead intrusion by opportunistic criminals. The attackers in these scenarios have almost nothing in common, and the proper response for each is very different.

If you spend your time preparing for the unlikely event, you leave yourself vulnerable to the more likely threat. It's a contrived comparison, but it illustrates the concept.

*Where is your dividing line?*

Ultimately you need to make decisions about what you're preparing for. Some events or kinds of incidents are going to be near certainties, some will be very likely, some a little less likely, some not-so-likely, and some which are downright improbable (but still, strictly speaking, possible.)

Naturally you should be preparing for the most likely events first. You'll need to consider what your homestead might face and rank them in terms of their likelihood. Once you've done that you can think about how you'd prepare to handle those events.

At some point, though, you'll reach a state of diminishing returns. As things become less and less likely, the resources you use to prepare for them (including your training and practice time) exceed the risk you face. Back to our paratroopers: unless you live next to a mall in South Korea, preparing for that event is really a waste of your time, effort, and money.

Where, then, is that dividing line — the one which separates those things that it makes sense to prepare for and those which are just a waste of resources? I'd say it's the plausibility line.

Plausible things are those which could happen because there is some historical basis for them happening. In other words, while they don't happen often enough to be certain or even mathematically likely, they've happened often enough that they could reasonably be believed to occur in your life.

They may also be the logical expected result of some foreseeable combination of events. In other words, they could reasonably be expected to happen under some specific set of circumstances.

### Why understanding expectation is important

It should be self-evident that no one has an unlimited amount of time, energy, money, and interest to train and equip for everything that is possible. You need to prioritize what you do in order to establish how to decide what skills to learn and practice.

Think of it like budgeting: You can't afford everything, so you need to decide what's important to you and spend your funds on those things first. It's the same idea.

If a scenario crosses that "plausible" line, if it's not believable given your life or environment, then perhaps spending resources preparing for it isn't the best idea. Focus on those things that are on the likely side of the plausible line.

### Skills have levels of expectation too

So far we've been talking about events or incidents, things that happen to you and affect what you train for. They help you budget your preparation resources: time, money, energy, and interest.

Your expectation of using a particular skill is also subject to the plausibility test. There are skills you might actually need, and then there are skills that fall into the range of merely possible (or, as I like to refer to it, "fantasyland"). Training in skills that fall beyond your plausibility line are likely a waste of your preparation resources.

For instance, the emergency (or "speed") rifle reload isn't a skill that's commonly needed. It's nearly impossible to find instances in private-sector self-defense where people needed to reload their defensive rifle. It's just not a skill people actually use; with the capacity and power of the rifle it's not something that could believably happen, and it's not really even the result of a set of a foreseeable combination of events. In other words, it fails most people's plausibility test.

Yet speed reloading takes up a lot of time in most defensive rifle shooting courses. I've seen instructors spend the better part of an hour on the topic, teaching several different reloading methods and doing specialized reloading drills, all for a skill that students will (if we're being honest) never need. This valuable and expensive instructional time could have been better used to teach the students how to make their first accurate shot happen faster — that's a skill of very high expectation and value.

Remember: there are no "advanced" defensive shooting skills. There are simply applications of fundamental skills over a wider range of plausible circumstances.

—

*\* - No, seriously: I had no idea this was a movie plot! I thought I was just unusually and uniquely creative when I came up with the storyline. Perhaps instead of writing self-defense books, I should write movie scripts?*

## Chapter Five
# RIFLES FOR PERIMETER DEFENSE

What rifles are suitable for perimeter defense?

Just about any rifle can be (and likely has been) pressed into service to protect your family and homestead. When necessity demands, you use the tools you have at hand without regard for their relative suitability.

That being said, if you're reading this book, you're at a point where you can plan and prepare for your "worst-case scenario." The beauty of preparation is that you can pick the best tool for the expected task ahead of time — and some rifles are simply more suitable than others.

## Rifle calibers

If you've been around the shooting community for any length of time, you probably already know the religious fervor that surrounds caliber selection. People get quite attached to their favorite cartridge and argue its merits, real or imagined, incessantly. (Some shooters will even champion what can only be considered odd or non-mainstream calibers, and to that I myself must confess some guilt!)

Let's take a look at some popular rifle calibers, ones you'll likely find at your local gun store, and consider their merits for the job of perimeter defense.

*Rimfire cartridges (.17HMR, .22 Long Rifle, .22 Magnum):* The various rimfire cartridges are among the most useful tools on the farm, ranch, or homestead. A better cartridge for small pests (and medium-sized pests at close range) cannot be found. They have light recoil, superb accuracy, and are chambered in light, easy-handling rifles. If the rimfire is the only rifle you have, it can certainly be pressed into service for this job. However, as I alluded to earlier, at this point it shouldn't be the only rifle you have — or at least, plan to have. The rimfire lacks the usable power and range of the centerfire cartridges discussed below and can't always reliably take down a determined attacker regardless of the number of legs involved. If you must out of necessity use a rimfire rifle for your perimeter defense, precisely aim your shots at the attacker's vital organs and fire multiple rounds as rapidly as possible until the attack ceases.

*.223 Remington (aka 5.56x45)\*:* Though it can be had in bolt-actions, the .223/5.56 round is most commonly chambered in the AR-15 pattern rifle, which of this writing is far and away the best-selling rifle in this country. That makes .223/5.56 ammunition the most popular rifle caliber in most stores, and it often sells out when demand goes up.

.223/5.56 ammunition is available in a wide variety of bullet weights and types to suit many different shooting tasks. As a perimeter defense round, the .223/5.56 is almost ideal, with good range, excellent terminal performance, superb accuracy, and light recoil. When chambered in modern autoloading rifles such as the AR-15 type, it really comes into its own. If your anticipated defensive needs include large predators such as bear, this round is not ideal, but for almost everything else, it's high on my "recommended" list.

*6.5 Creedmoor:* The 6.5 CM, as it's often referred to, is currently one of the most popular chamberings for high-accuracy bolt-action rifles and is becoming more common in semiautomatic firearms. The 6.5mm caliber Creedmoor possesses superb accuracy at extremely long ranges and is a favorite of competitive target shooters. Because of its popularity, it's also becoming an increasingly common hunting round, and boasts a large ammunition selection. When loaded with appropriate bullets, there is very little the 6.5 CM can't handle. Although the guns that chamber the round are larger and heavier than the ubiquitous AR-15, they're still handy and would make a good perimeter defense choice. (The .260 Remington, which is also a 6.5mm cartridge and ballistically nearly identical to the Creedmoor but in a slightly larger case, would be a good alternative that is chambered in a wider range of rifles.)

*.30 Carbine:* The .30 Carbine is almost synonymous with the rifle for which it was designed, the famous M1 Carbine of World War II. The .30 Carbine is nearly the exclusive province of that rifle, though after the war a few attempts were made to chamber the round in lever-action and bolt-action rifles; neither effort met with much success. The .30 Carbine garnered something of a split reputation during the war, with some praising its performance and others deriding it as ineffective against determined adversaries. The reality probably lies somewhere in the middle, but in all fairness, the beauty of the .30 Carbine is really in the light, short, fast-handling rifle that chambered it. The Carbine round suffers from a lack of good defensive ammunition. Only a few suitable loads are available, and they can be difficult to find. The Carbine exhibits a severe drop in performance as range increases, but within its range (say, 50 to 75 yards) and loaded with appropriate ammo, it can be a workable choice for perimeter defense. However, I generally recommend relegating the Carbine to the role in which it really shines — defense inside the home.

*.300 Blackout:* Precisely termed the .300 AAC Blackout for its invention by the American Armament Corporation, the .300 BLK, as it's often abbreviated, was designed primarily to gain maximum performance on a rifle with a suppressor ("silencer") attached. But it has proven to be a

superb hunting round fired from unsuppressed rifles. It has become one of the most common choices for hunting feral hogs in the southern part of the United States, a role in which it excels. It is most commonly chambered in semiautomatic rifles, particularly of the AR-15 pattern, and should be well suited to the task of perimeter defense.

*7.62x39:* Most popularly known as the "7.62 Soviet," this is the round chambered by the Russian AK and SKS firearms that have become so popular in this country. The 7.62x39mm cartridge is roughly equal in power to our own (much older) .30-30 Winchester but suffers from a lack of ammunition selection. If loaded with soft-point or hollow-point bullets, the Soviet round would make a suitable perimeter defense choice, but accuracy is always a question given the construction quality of the rifles in which it is typically chambered. Ammunition quality is also often a question, and foreign hollow-point bullets usually are such in name only. They do not perform like the hollow-point or soft-point ammunition we're accustomed to using in our rifles. If this is your choice, I strongly recommend sticking to American-produced ammunition for defensive use (the imported stuff being fine for practice).

*.30-30 Winchester:* The .30-30 dates clear back to 1895 and was at one time the most common deer-hunting companion across the U.S., particularly in states west of the Mississippi. For many westerners, the .30-30 was their first hunting arm and the first "real" rifle they were taught to shoot. Although there have been a few bolt-action rifles chambered for this accomplished cartridge, the vast majority of .30-30 rifles have been light, fast-handling lever-action carbines. The long history of the .30-30 means a wide selection of ammunition is available at just about any gun or sporting goods store. While the .30-30 isn't considered a long-range cartridge, it's more than adequate for use inside the distances we'll consider in perimeter defense. The guns that chamber the round have the advantage of being as politically correct as any rifle can be and are usually available in jurisdictions that make owning semiauto rifles difficult. While it's not ideal in any one cate-

gory, its combination of adequate performance, good handling, and ubiquity may make it the best choice for some people in some circumstances.

*.308 Winchester:* Say "three-oh-eight" and most people know you're talking about the .308 Winchester. It's one of the most popular and widespread rifle cartridges made and the basis for the 7.62x51mm NATO round used by militaries all over the world. It's used for everything from big-game hunting to competition shooting to military sniping. It offers good power, tolerable recoil, and renowned accuracy with a wide range of bullet weights, and is available in bolt-action, lever-action, and semiautomatic rifles. The .308 is effective well beyond the range needed for perimeter defense, and bullets must be carefully selected to minimize "shoot through" at the defensive ranges we'll be exploring. It is, in my estimation, at the top end of ballistic power needed for defensive uses.

*.30-06 Springfield:* While ".308" can describe both a specific cartridge and a common bullet diameter, the term "ought-six" describes but one thing: the .30-06 Springfield cartridge. The .30-06 went into service with our military in 1906 and was our primary small-arms caliber through both World Wars, the Korean War, and saw limited use during the Vietnam War — and is still use by some armies around the globe. It is also one of our most popular sporting cartridges, being chambered in a wide range of bolt-action rifles used by hunters all over the world. It is a large, powerful cartridge, but with lighter bullets (to minimize range and overpenetration) may be pressed into service as a perimeter defense round. Still, from weight, power, and recoil standpoints, it is far more than is needed and is not my first choice for the job.

*Magnum cartridges:* There is no specific definition of "magnum" that everyone agrees on (or that is universally applicable), but it's generally held to be a cartridge that results from enlarging an existing (or parent) cartridge to hold more gunpowder and deliver more power. Magnum cartridges are designed for long-range performance or for large, dangerous game animals. Such extreme performance comes at the cost of size, weight, high recoil, and significant muzzle blast. With only a few exceptions (most of which are covered below), magnum cartridges are not recommended for perimeter defense. (Of course any rifle can be pressed into service in an emergency, but I'll reiterate: Since we have the luxury of planning and preparing ahead of our need for the tool, we can choose something more suitable.)

*Pistol calibers:* Many rifles are chambered in cartridges we normally associate with handguns. You can, for instance, find rifles chambered in 9mm Luger (Parabellum) and .45ACP, two very popular defensive pistol calibers. These are normally referred to not as rifles, but as "pistol-caliber carbines" or "PCC." I'm a proponent of PCCs as in-home defensive tools due to their accuracy, ease of handling, and extremely light recoil and muzzle blast. But as perimeter defense tools, they usually leave something to be desired in terms of range: beyond 50 yards or so, they run out of power very rapidly. Making a humane shot on a predatory animal at 75 or 100 yards is less sure than with almost any rifle round.

There are some exceptions to this, and they're also exceptions to my rule about magnum cartridges. Many rifles have been chambered in the .357 and .44 Magnum revolver rounds, and they make nearly ideal perimeter defense choices. They have good range — a little more than 100 yards for the .357 and considerably more for the .44 — and relatively mild recoil compared to most rifle rounds. The .357 is particularly light in recoil and muzzle blast, and has more than enough power for any plausible defensive scenario against human criminal or animal marauder. (If you need protection against dangerous bears, the .44 Magnum rifle might be a better choice. Very few people fall into that category.) Both rounds have been chambered in bolt-action rifles, but they're usually associated with short, light, lever-action carbines. One of my personal perimeter defense rifles, in fact, is a .357 lever-action. I've used it on both game and predatory animals and have been impressed with its performance in each case.

**Rifle types**

If you're new to the world of rifles, you may find the choices overwhelming. So many different designs and sizes — how do you choose among them?

Rifles come in several different action types. The action refers to the operating parts of the rifle that feed and fire the ammunition, and while there have been many different designs over the years, manufacturers have settled on just a few basic types.

*Bolt-action:* The bolt-action rifle is a manually operated action common on hunting and sharpshooting rifles, and the most common military rifle design up through World War II. The bolt-action has a handle that the shooter lifts up and pulls back to eject a spent cartridge, then pushes forward and down to chamber a round and prepare for firing. With practice, a bolt-action rifle can be fairly fast to operate, but most people find the bolt-action a little slow and clumsy. Bolt-action rifles can be chambered in a huge range of cartridges, from the least powerful to the most powerful on earth, and are usually renowned for their accuracy. While a bolt-action would not usually be my first choice as a perimeter defense tool, it can — with careful selection — be a workable choice for those who commit to learning and practicing its operation. The various "Scout Rifle" configurations, most notably those from Steyr Arms, are the best choice of the type.

*Lever-action:* If you've ever seen a western movie, you've seen lever-action rifles in abundance! The lever-action is often called a "cowboy rifle," largely because of its association with the settling of the American west. The lever-action feeds ammunition from its magazine (which is usually a tube under the barrel) by way of swinging its lever down and forward. The lever-action is faster to operate than the bolt-action, especially for the less experienced shooter. It's chambered in a lesser range of cartridges than its bolt-action cousins, but the available chamberings cover all the ranges we'll consider in perimeter defense. Lever-action rifles tend to be short, slim, light, and very handy and thus make superb choices as defensive tools — even if some people consider them out of date!

*Semiautomatic:* The semiautomatic rifle, often referred to as "semiauto" or simply "semi," is more properly referred to as self-loading. The first round is loaded by hand; when that round is fired, the gun uses part of the energy generated by the round to eject the spent casing, cock the gun, and chamber a new round in anticipation for another shot. When the trigger is pulled, the round fires and the process is repeated. This is different from a fully automatic rifle, where rounds are fired and reloaded continuously when the trigger is held down; in a semiauto, only one round is fired for each pull of the trigger. The semiauto is the most popular type of rifle sold today, and the common AR-15 is an excellent example of the design. The semiauto usually has a greater ammunition capacity than any other rifle type and is more easily reloaded — features that are often touted as important for defensive purposes, even though examples of that capability actually being used in a private-sector defensive encounter are quite difficult to find.

*Single shot:* Before any of those other rifle designs came into being, the single-shot rifle reigned supreme. The single-shot rifle carries no additional ammunition and must be reloaded by hand after every shot. Single-shot rifles have a variety of operating mechanisms, but all have one thing in common: they're slow and quite difficult to use, even for experienced shooters, especially when the heart is racing and hands are trembling. While I can find reasons to use any of the other rifles described, I cannot in good conscience recommend a single-shot rifle for any defensive use except in an emergency where there are no other options.

## Barrel lengths

Rifles are commonly made with barrel lengths from 16 (the federally mandated minimum length**) to 28 inches. The longer barrels are typically used for the Magnum-class cartridges and usually on rifles destined for target/competition shooting, where portability and weight are secondary concerns. Most of the rifles suitable for defensive use typically come with barrels between 16 and 20 inches.

### *What's a carbine?*

In the days when military rifles with barrels of 30 inches were not uncommon, the need was felt for shorter, easier-to-handle arms. For example, mounted cavalry found it difficult to use a long rifle from horseback. Military armories would make (or have made) rifles with shorter barrels to accommodate those and other special uses. The change in length was sometimes dramatic — the Swedish army at one time issued rifles with 30-inch barrels and carbines with very short (for the day) 18-inch barrels.

So the carbine was nothing more than a shortened rifle, but over time, shorter guns that had no larger counterpart were produced. The U.S. M1 Carbine of World War II, for instance, had no rifle equivalent. Today, a carbine has generally come to mean any long arm with a barrel of less than 18 inches, or any long arm chambered in a smaller cartridge regardless of barrel length (see the previous entry about "pistol calibers"). In any case, a carbine is a light, short, handy rifle ideal for the job of perimeter defense!

### *Bullpup rifles*

Making a carbine from a rifle by simply reducing the barrel length brings with it certain issues, one of which has to do with ballistics. The shorter the barrel, the less velocity the bullet develops and the less power it brings to the target. When barrel lengths become extremely short, ballistic performance can be so compromised that the bullets cannot reliably do their job. It's a tradeoff between portability and performance.

The bullpup rifle design attempts to get the best of both worlds by redesigning the entire rifle for ultimate compactness. In a conventional rifle, the action of the gun sits in the stock well in front of the shooter; the shooter's face is behind the action and barrel. In a bullpup design, the action is moved rearward so that it is against (or nearly so) the shooter's shoulder, and the shooter's cheek rests on top of the action. This design can cut a foot or more off of the total length of the rifle. A bullpup with a full-length rifle barrel is the same length as a conventional carbine with a cut-down barrel. This gives the ballistic performance of a full-size rifle in the package of a carbine — and a very small carbine, to boot!

This type of rifle is not new, though it is not tremendously popular in the United States. The militaries of Austria, Israel, Great Britain, and France have all issued bullpup rifles to their troops over the last 40+ years, but they have not caught on in this country with either the military or civilian gun owners.

The largest impediment seems to be cost: A bullpup rifle is often 50% more expensive than its conventional counterpart, and in some cases can be double the cost. This pricing discrepancy, along with being caught in the 1994 "assault rifle" ban (which expired in 2004), reduced bullpup demand in this country to a small percentage of total rifle sales.

Today bullpups from several manufacturers are widely available, but the pricing differentials remain. They're typically found in the hands of bullpup enthusiasts who don't mind paying extra to get the compact and maneuverable qualities bullpups are known for.

I was not a fan of the bullpup until I spent a couple of years using a Steyr AUG, the world's most successful bullpup rifle. I discovered that its handling characteristics made the bullpup an excellent choice for the job of perimeter defense. One of the salient aspects of this kind of defensive use is that the rifle has to be retrieved from its storage space and moved to be used. It's not regularly carried like the defensive handgun, nor perpetually on a sling like a long gun carried by a police officer or infantryman who is patrolling. The perimeter defense rifle has to be retrieved from wherever it's stored, readied for action quickly, and then taken to the point where it will actually be employed.

This means that, in the worst-case scenario, the rifle might need to be maneuvered from storage to use through a room, then a doorway, then down a hall, then through another doorway and another room, and finally a doorway to the outside. It might mean taking the rifle around furniture or needing to open doors, not to mention the presence of other people. Having an extremely compact rifle makes that maneuvering faster, easier, and safer for all concerned. That is almost the perfect use for the short bullpup configuration.

Handling while shooting is also different with the bullpup. The weight is centered roughly over the shooting hand, as opposed to most rifles, which have a decidedly barrel-heavy weight distribution. This change in the center of mass enhances the ability to swing the rifle to target and still be able to stop quickly when aligned on a threat.

There's a lot more to talk about with the bullpup rifle, but suffice it to say that if you have the financial means, you should consider one for your perimeter defense needs.

### Is high capacity a real concern?

I'm quite fond of the 30-round magazines that fit in my AR-15 rifle. I'm fond of the 20-round magazines that fit it, too. I would not want to give those up to a changing political landscape and understand the reason other responsible gun owners fight the efforts to regulate or outright ban magazines based on capacity.

At the same time, integrity compels me to admit I'd be quite comfortable with a defensive rifle that holds far less ammunition. Can I defend myself with a rifle that only holds five or eight rounds of ammunition? Yes, I can — and countless others have over at least two centuries.

As mentioned earlier, we use a rifle for perimeter defense because of its increased capabilities over a handgun. The increased range, power, and precision of the rifle make it much more likely to end the fight very quickly. When you consider that even handguns almost always end the incident with whatever ammunition they contain, regardless of how many rounds that actually is, it's hard to argue that the rifle will do less.

I wouldn't want to face, nor do I recommend facing, threats with a single-shot rifle. At the same time, I don't feel that 30 rounds are absolutely necessary either. Somewhere in the middle (and I use the term "middle" quite loosely) is the point of sufficiency. I submit for your consideration that the actual figure attached to "sufficient" is probably smaller than you've been led to believe.

You need to decide for yourself what you're comfortable with. What I can tell you is that, after several decades of study and a few experiences of my own, I really don't worry about capacity any longer. It would be hard to find a rifle today that doesn't have sufficient capacity for the job of perimeter defense.

**Modifying your rifle**

Before the modular AR-15/AR-10-pattern rifle became ubiquitous, rifle modifications were few and far between. A dedicated target shooter might replace the trigger with a much lighter precision unit, and some people had custom stocks made, but beyond that, modifications required a talented gunsmith, time, and a not-inconsiderable amount of money.

The AR-15 changed all that. Any modification you might want to do to an AR-pattern rifle can be done in your garage with relatively simple tools. Most of them can be accomplished on your kitchen table\*\*\*.

Other than sights, though, modifications to a defensive rifle should be entertained only after thorough consideration. With only a few exceptions, I could quite easily and successfully use any off-the-shelf rifle for perimeter defense — and so could you.

For example, a perimeter defense rifle really doesn't need a super-light "target" trigger. Even the heavy triggers in most bullpup rifles do not preclude sufficiently precise shooting out to 100 yards or so, which is about the limit of justifiable and humane defense. I haven't handled a new semiautomatic or bolt-action rifle with a trigger anywhere near as bad as the average bullpup rifle, which means replacement triggers just aren't all that important.

I caution against replacing or working on your rifle's trigger. When you're out of breath and shaking from fear is not the time to try to deal with a too-light trigger, the consequences of which can be an unintended shot. Save the target triggers for the calmness of the shooting range.

If you have a conventionally stocked rifle and short arms, having the butt shortened may be a good investment. I have very short arms for an adult male (a consequence of being 5' 6" tall on a good day) and often have issues comfortably shooting some rifles. Many of mine feature so-called "youth" stocks or regular stocks that have been shortened to fit me. I consider it a worthwhile modification.

If you have an AR-15-style rifle, pay attention to the pistol grip. While most rifles today come with very serviceable grips that allow you to get your hand into an optimal shooting position, some are still equipped with the standard A2-style grip, which features a shelf between the middle and ring fingers. That shelf is placed in an odd position for many shooters and doesn't allow the trigger finger to move optimally****. Replacing the grip makes shooting the AR-15 more pleasant and consistent for many people.

Beyond those things, modifications to the rifle don't do much to aid the job of perimeter defense. I suggest investing the funds that would have been so spent on more ammunition and training. You'll get more "bang for your buck" in terms of your ability to protect yourself and your family.

—

\* - *Purists will point out that there are some technical differences between the .223 (civilian) and 5.56mm (military) versions of this cartridge, but in terms of application and performance, they are essentially identical. The main concern is safety: While .223 Remington ammunition can be safely fired in a gun marked for 5.56, doing the opposite can result in an unsafe condition. For more information, see:*

*www.americanrifleman.org/articles/2013/3/4/223-remington-vs-556-whats-in-a-name/*

\*\* - *Cutting a barrel to less than 16 inches in length or manufacturing a rifle with such a barrel, is a federal crime unless the gun is registered as a "short - barreled rifle" (SBR) and a federal tax of $200 is paid. The applicant must also submit to a thorough background check and notify the chief law enforcement officer in his or her area of the existence of the gun. In addition, there are restrictions on the transport and resale of such items. Is there any wonder why I'm a fan of the legally shorter bullpup rifle?*

\*\*\* - *In the interest of family harmony, I suggest discussing this ahead of time with your significant other. Some people simply have no sense of humor where such things are concerned.*

\*\*\*\* - *Back in the days before there was a robust aftermarket for these rifles, we used to take a rotary tool and grind away that little shelf. The difference in handling was immediately apparent. Interestingly, we were in fact turning our A2 grips into the previous A1 style, with which the original M16 rifles were equipped. They had it right the first time!*

## Chapter Six
## SIGHTING OPTIONS

With good physical alignment and consistent handling, it's possible to hit targets a few yards away without using any sighting devices. But once you get past that "close-quarters battle" range, you're going to need some form of sighting device in order to reliably hit your target with your rifle. That part of the equation isn't really debatable: To use the rifle at the distances for which it was designed, you need some sort of sight.

What form the sighting device should take is a subject of considerable argument in the shooting community, with everyone having their personal favorite that they defend enthusiastically. In reality, any of the common sighting systems will work for the job of perimeter defense, but some are more efficient or easier to use in a wider range of conditions.

### Iron sights

The sights that come on most rifles, typically consisting of a post or ramp in front and a notch or peephole at the rear, are collectively called iron sights* or "irons." Iron sights have been around almost since the birth of the rifle and are often the first sighting system new shooters learn to use.

Though they may seem quaint in the era of electronic and optical sights, irons still have several advantages. First is ubiquity: Most, though certainly not all, rifles come from the factory with some form of iron sights.

Since they're already installed, there's no extra cost for a rifle that can be put to use immediately. The concepts of sight alignment (when the front and rear are in proper relationship with each other) and sight picture (when the aligned sights are properly placed on the target) are the same between rifle and handgun, giving some commonality between the two and making use of your already existing skills.

Iron sights are also quite durable and reliable; they have no batteries to worry about nor lenses to keep clean. Iron sights don't fog up like optical sights can, and aren't affected by rain or dust. They have a low profile, which means less snagging when handling the rifle rapidly or in close quarters. They're also lightweight. Some optical sights add a significant amount of weight to a rifle, weight that's well above the center of gravity and makes the rifle less maneuverable.

A big advantage to many people, including yours truly, is that iron sights have no "magnification tremble." Many people using optical sights (scopes), even those of low magnification, find the increased visibility of rifle movement distracting — to the point that it affects accuracy. I find the apparent lack of tremble makes it easier to keep the sights aligned on target for a precision shot.**

That said, iron sights do have some disadvantages. One of the biggest is that their usability declines in direct proportion to any change in eyesight. Precision shooting, particularly at distance, requires the ability to focus on the front sight. As eyes age, their ability to focus at close objects declines, and the ability to rapid shift their focus also deteriorates. Iron sights rely on the flexibility inherent in the human eye, which means they become increasingly more difficult to use over time.

Another disadvantage is that, because iron sights have two different focus points — the target and the front sight — you can't keep them both sharp at the same time. You need to decide which needs the most attention at the moment, and if your attention is focused on the front sight, you can't watch your threat. Determining if you need to shoot, or need to keep shooting, is made more difficult. Later in the book, I'll show you some techniques to minimize the discrepancy, but the iron sight will always be at a disadvantage for threat focus as the range increases.

Finally, it's just more difficult to hit small targets, or targets at a distance, with iron sights. If you've encountered a rabid animal, as I have, and are forced to shoot at a longer distance to avoid any chance of contact, you'll find the iron sights much harder to use. This is particularly true if the target is small, at an inopportune angle, or partially obscured.

Though I like iron sights -- I've used them my entire life, and one of my perimeter defense rifles is equipped with irons -- I must acknowledge their disadvantages in the aforementioned areas. However, it's possible, particularly if you're younger and have better eyesight than I do, that an iron-equipped rifle will serve you completely adequately for the job of perimeter defense.

*Types of iron sights*

Iron sights come in a wide range of configurations, with each manufacturer having a slightly different take on any given style.

*There are many variations in rifle sights, far too many to show here. These represent commonly encountered versions of (left to right) notch-and-post, peep (or ghost ring), full buckhorn, and express sights.*

*Notch and post:* Most iron rifle sights are of the notch-and-post variety familiar to handgun shooters. Sometimes referred to as "flat-top" sights, notch-and-post sights are aligned so the top of the front sight is even with the flat top of the rear sight and an even amount of space is on either side of the front sight. The spot on the target that you want to hit is placed on top of and centered on the front sight.

Many rifle sights are some variation of this combination. The most common variant has a round ball or bead in the front sight and a "U"-shaped notch in the rear sight. In use, the front sight is nestled in the matching rear notch, again with the desired target point on top of the front sight.

*Express sights:* These are an extreme variant of notch-and-post sights. The express sight, as its name implies, is designed for ultimate speed over precision. Express sights have their origins in the world of dangerous game hunting, where it may be necessary to make a very fast shot on an animal that is in the midst of a defensive attack against its pursuer.

The express sight consists of a very shallow "V"-shaped trench on the rear sight and a somewhat large bead or ball on the front sight. In use, the ball is placed at the bottom of the "V" and then pointed at the target. That gives a coarse yet sufficient alignment for very fast and close shooting. With practice, the apex of the ball can be used for more precise shooting, just as it would be with the bead-and-"U"-notch variety. But the imprecise positioning of the ball in the trench and the large size of the ball limit the achievable precision. (Some particularly talented shooters can do remarkable things with express sights, but I am not one of them!)

*Buckhorn sights:* Back in the days when muzzleloaders were still common and self-contained metallic cartridges were the leading edge of technology, the buckhorn sight ruled the roost. The buckhorn, so named because the shape of the rear sight mimicked the curve of a mature buck's antlers, was conceived as a way of compensating for the extreme drop of the bullets used in those low-velocity arms. The idea was to use the bottom notch — which is quite similar to today's notch-and-post sights — for close shots, and align the front sight between the "horns" of the sight for long distance shots. That extreme change in elevation compensated for the drop of the bullet.

With today's better cartridges, the need for the buckhorn has declined. Only a very few rifles still come equipped with them, those rifles mostly being nostalgic versions of the lever-action. Buckhorn sights are, however, found on many used rifles.

*Peeps and ghost rings:* Peep and so-called "ghost ring" sights are closely related. In both, you look through a circular opening on the rear sight and align the front sight in the center of the circle. It's actually quite easy to do, because your mind has a tendency to center things in circles. As a result, the front sight almost seems to self-align as you're looking at it through the hole in the rear.

The smaller the hole in the rear peep, the greater the potential precision. At the same time, a smaller hole lets in less light, which makes a small peep sight very difficult to use as the light level decreases. Military peep sights tend to be larger than target or competition peep sights, and the famous M16 rifle originally came equipped with a flip-over dual peep. One leg had a large hole, for shooting fast or in lower light, and the other leg had a smaller hole for more precise shooting at longer ranges.

The ghost ring is a peep sight with a large hole and a relatively thin ring around the circle. The ghost ring is popular on defensive shotguns, where the range limitations of the shells make slightly reduced precision a minor issue. Ghost rings have been attached to rifles for fast shooting in low light or at short distances. The M16 large peep mentioned earlier is much closer to a ghost ring than many of its contemporaries.

A peep sight with a large hole has a lot to recommend it as a perimeter defense sighting system. Properly chosen, it can provide the necessary precision at longer ranges and still be quite usable at closer distances, as well as in reduced lighting conditions.

*Tang sights:* A peep or ghost ring sight must be mounted close to the eye to work properly. The peep needs to be very out of focus to force the seemingly automatic alignment that makes them so useful. On guns where the rear sight is mounted to the barrel, the peep or ghost ring doesn't work as well because the distance from the eye doesn't allow for the required blur. (This is also why they don't work on pistols, where the rear sight is also far from the eye.) In the days when lever-action rifles were the most popular choice, this problem was handled by a device known as a tang sight.

The tang sight is nothing more than a peep sight mounted on a short stalk that attaches to the tang of the rifle, behind the hammer, where most people curl their shooting thumb over the stock. This places the peep very close to the eye, where it needs to be, to increase the precision capability of the rifle. Tang sights have fallen greatly out of favor, and although they're still made and sold, their inherent fragility makes them a poor choice for a rifle that might get knocked around in an emergency.

*Front sight configurations*

The front sights found on rifles today tend to come in two main styles. The first is a simple post with a squared-off top. This is common on guns like the AR-15. Looking through the sights, the shooter sees a rectangle, the top of which is the area where the bullet should hit if the sights are adjusted properly. This sight can also take the form of a simple ramp. The view from the shooter's perspective is the same, because it's the outline seen through the rear sight.

The other style, more common on lever- and bolt-action rifles, features a bead or dot on top of a narrow blade. The effect is sometimes called a "lollipop sight," because from the shooter's position, the front sight looks like the silhouette of a lollipop on a stick. The bead or dot is sometimes made of a light-colored material such as brass or white plastic, so the sight is more visible when light hits it. If the light is in front of the shooter, the sight presents the lollipop silhouette.

The size of the front sight can vary considerably, and in most cases is easily changed. A wider post or a larger bead is easier to see when lighting conditions aren't optimal. A smaller post or bead lends itself to more precise shooting at longer distances. The choice depends on you and your eyesight, with some consideration given to the maximum expected range where you might need to shoot.

*Are iron sights suitable for perimeter defense?*

Some maintain that, given the prevalence of modern optical and electronic sights, iron sights are obsolete. They would argue that iron sights are a remnant of a distant past when irons were the only choice for a defensive rifle.

The argument has some merit but ignores the fact that iron sights still work as well as they ever did. Yes, in some cases modern sighting systems have definite advantages. Iron sights, however, didn't stop working when those new sights were invented!

Iron sights require a bit more training time and effort to learn to use properly, but they can still be used to great effect. In my house, we have a mix of iron and optical sights, and I find the iron sights to have far fewer drawbacks than they are commonly believed to have.

Plus, they're free!

## Conventional optical sights (scopes)

It's rare today to find a hunting rifle that's not equipped with a scope, a magnifying optic that uses a reticle (a fine alignment grid or mark) placed on the same visual plane as the target.

When you look through iron sights, it's clear that the front sight and the target are not in the same plane because you must choose which to focus on. The scope, on the other hand, eliminates that problem by optically making the reticle appear as though it's right on the target. Your eye sees the reticle as being on the same plane as the target and eliminating the choice of which to focus on — because both the reticle and the target are in focus.

With both in focus, you can observe and aim at the same time without shifting your focus point. This ability to observe and aim is, in my estimation, the biggest benefit of an optical sight (and of the electronic sight discussed below).

After all, if we're going to use our rifles for the job of defense, it's our responsibility to know when we can shoot and when we need to stop shooting. The only way we can make those decisions is if we have information about what the threat is doing. The only way to get that information is to be focused on the threat. The optical sight makes this possible without compromising shooting performance.

In the not-too-distant past***, scopes were considered fragile items. The avid hunter was always advised to leave the iron sights on his rifle and to equip his scope with a quick-release mechanism, in the event the scope was damaged and a shot presented itself. Over the years, however, manufacturers have constantly improved the ruggedness and durability of their scopes — to the point that a quality optic, in my estimation, is easily as durable as the iron sights on which we historically relied.

This has been borne out over the past few decades of warfare around the world. When Steyr Arms introduced their AUG rifle in the 1970s, they included a permanently mounted optic in lieu of iron sights. The move was widely denigrated in shooting publications, but their gamble proved to be the winning one. Soldiers were able to take advantage of the enhanced precision of their optics with very few failures. Today, it's rare to see a rifle in a combat area that doesn't have some sort of optical or electronic sighting system.

Today's scopes are so well made and reliable, even under severe conditions, that I consider "back-up" sights to be superfluous. A quality scope will probably outlast you and me, combined!

**Electronic sights**

In the past decade, the electronic (or more precisely, electro-optical) sight has exploded in popularity. It is now the preferred sighting system for competitive, law enforcement, and military shooters.

An electronic sight, usually referred to as a "red dot," combines a non-magnifying optical system and a simple reticle that, like conventional scopes, is on the same optical plane as the target. The reticle is usually red (though green versions are now becoming available) and is often nothing more than a large dot in the center of the field of view — hence the term red dot.

*Red-dot design*

Red-dot scopes are a marvel of modern technology. They use an LED array to form the reticle, then project the reticle forward to the back side of the objective (front) lens. Special coatings on that lens are tuned to the wavelengths of the LED array and reflect the image of the reticle back to the shooter's eye. This reflection mechanism leads to the less common but more accurate descriptive term "reflex sight."

Reflex sights come in two major design variations — open and tube. The open sights resemble the heads-up display panel in a fighter jet. There is one lens, the objective, mounted forward in a skeleton frame. The LED array is on the back side of that lens and below it. The reticle is projected up and forward to reflect off the back side of the objective lens to be viewed by the shooter.

The tube type has the optics and electronics mounted in a metal cylinder, somewhat reminiscent of a conventional optical sight. The tube sight has an objective (front) lens as well as a rear lens, which exists primarily to seal the tube. In the tube design, the LED array is usually mounted to one side, allowing the entire optic to be shorter in height and mount closer to the rifle.

Each design has advantages and disadvantages. The open style is less confining to look through than the tube style. It feels more like looking through a window than through a scope. The view is less obscured, making it easy to see the surrounding area even when aimed at a target.

Many shooters maintain the open style is faster to get on target, because the design is more tolerant of the shooter's eye being off-axis than is the tube style. The open sight can also be made smaller and lighter without a significant penalty in usability.

On the other hand, the tube-style sights are usually more reliable than the open variety, particularly in harsh conditions. The tube style's LED array is sealed inside, where dust and water can't get to it. In contrast, the LEDs of the open sights can be obscured by dirt and reduce the visibility of the reticle. The open sight's unprotected objective lens is often criticized for its exposure and fragility, while the protective housing of the tube style seems to better protect the optics.

*Pros and cons of reflex sights*

The red dot's distinct advantages are speed and ease of use. Like a conventional scope, the reticle is projected to the same optical plane as the target. The shooter can watch the target and maintain aim at the same time. All the shooter needs to do is find the dot, point it at the target, and the bullet will hit where the dot is pointed.

Because of the non-magnifying optics, it's easy to leave both eyes open while aiming, enabling the shooter to keep watch on his or her surroundings. You can imagine the value to a soldier either in open terrain or clearing a terrorist stronghold, where being able to keep both eyes open for the enemy is a decided advantage. It's no wonder red-dot sights are found on a large percentage of the rifles in war zones today.

The biggest downside to the reflex sight is its overall reliability. Don't get me wrong: These sights are remarkably well built, but they do have some vulnerabilities. The optics, particularly in the tube design, are very rugged, but the electronics are still a weak point and can suffer damage from physical shock, extreme temperature changes, and simple component failure.

The majority of these optics are battery dependent, and while dead batteries are a maintenance issue and easily avoided, the contacts those batteries make to get their electrons to the circuitry can corrode or simply fail to make solid contact. The result can be a sporadic reticle image or even complete darkness.

I've seen reflex sight failures even in the relative calm of a shooting class. Unlike with a conventional optical sight, if the reticle in a red dot fails, the sight is useless. No battery power, no reticle, no aiming. For this reason, backup iron sights are strongly recommended with any reflex sight.

*Eyesight problems*

Another issue with the reflex sight occurs with shooters who have astigmatism. This eyesight defect, caused by irregularities in the curvature of the eye's lens, causes light rays from different parts of the lens to come to different points of focus on the retina. The result is distorted vision.

The nature of the reflected light from the LED array makes the projected reticle appear distorted to someone with astigmatism. Instead of being round, it might look like an irregular star or the swoosh from the well-known athletic shoe maker. Even with eyeglasses or contacts, people with astigmatism can find the red-dot optic anywhere from annoying to downright unusable.

Some red-dot sights pass the LED light through a holographic lens to project a more complex reticle than just a red dot. These sights are particularly sensitive to astigmatics, causing the reticle to be partially out of focus and often with a halo. Like many people, I suffer from astigmatism. Most red dots are slightly distorted to me, but I can usually work around the issue. But sights that use holographic projections are so distorted as to be unusable — plus, they give me a severe headache after a short period of time.

*Hybrid reflexes*

In an attempt to get around the issues with electronic failures of reflex sights, some manufacturers have attempted to build reflex sights using tritium (a glowing gas commonly used in night sights on handguns) to serve as the illumination source for the reticle. These sights have not proven terribly popular, as the faint glow of the tritium requires different coatings on the objective lens to reflect more light back to the shooter's eye. Those coatings make the view through the sight very dim and off-color compared to their battery-powered cousins. In all the training courses I've taught or attended, I've seen only a few of this design. The users of those sights were at a disadvantage when light levels declined in the afternoon of class, particularly on ranges where the targets were in shade while the shooters were still in sunlight.

---

*\*- Some people refer to these as "open sights," but technically, the term excludes peepholes and ghost rings, which are enclosed. All open sights are classified as irons, but not all irons are open!*

*\*\* - For many years, I had a pair of otherwise identical .22 target rifles, one equipped with a quality 4x scope and the other with a good set of precision iron sights of the target/peep variety. Even at 50 yards, which is not a long distance, I could consistently shoot much better with the irons than the scope. Having grown up using nothing but iron sights, I found the bouncing of the reticle suffi-*

*ciently disconcerting that I couldn't concentrate on all the other things necessary for precision shooting. I had to spend some time training myself to use the optical sights!*

\*\*\* - *More specifically, my not-too-distant past! Many readers will have grown up in an age of nothing but rugged, high-quality scopes. Never before have we had such a selection of durable optics from which to choose.*

*Chapter Seven*

# THE UTILITY RIFLE

In many rural households, particularly those where the inhabitants are not "gun people," a rifle is often called upon as a tool for a wide variety of purposes, from putting down sick animals to hunting to perimeter defense. A premium is placed on versatility — utility — over specialization.

I grew up in such a household. On our farm, we had our .22 rifle for small pest control, our shotgun for bird hunting, and the lever-action rifle to take care of everything else. This was common in the rural area where we lived, and is still common in many parts of the country even today.

In this chapter, we'll discuss the utility or multi-purpose rifle and why it may (or may not) be a concept you should consider.

## The appeal of versatility

There is much to be said for the virtue of wide application. First, of course, is economy. Guns and accessories are expensive, and the fewer of them you need to buy, the more money you have left over for other preparedness resources.

In my book *Prepping for Life,* I go into this concept in depth, but the simple explanation is that it's important to remember you probably have a lot of risks you should be preparing for — and limited resources with which to prepare. Spending lots of money on many different guns, each optimized for a very narrow range of application, doesn't increase your overall preparedness or safety. Putting together a rifle for a very specific but very unlikely event is a further waste of your resources.

Second, the rifle you're most familiar with is what you'll likely grab when you recognize the need for one. If you have a rifle set up for home defense but you spend most of your practice time with a different gun, the one you'll grab is the one you're used to using. A utility rifle, because of its application to a wide range of shooting problems, will naturally be the one you're likely to use most often, the one you become most comfortable with, and therefore the one you'll likely use most efficiently when you desperately need it.

Familiarity doesn't breed contempt — it breeds proficiency.

### What is a utility rifle?

A rifle selected and equipped to perform more than one specialized task, and do each acceptably well, can properly be termed a utility rifle. In today's society, such a rifle might be usable for perimeter defense, hunting, and perhaps even defense inside the home. These are all very different applications, and the rifle that can be pressed into service for all will necessitate some compromises.

If your rifle will be used for more than one specific task, carefully managing those compromises is important. You need to balance the rifle's capabilities with the actual tasks it will be asked to perform, and accept those limitations that do not materially affect its performance.

### The rifle

When most people consider a rifle for defensive use, thoughts immediately go to the semiautomatic action. Rapidity of fire is often deemed to be the most important feature for self-defense, and the semiauto is the king of rapid fire. The longer the distances involved, many would opine, the less important the rate of fire becomes.

In hunting, it's almost always considered a non-issue because follow-up shots, if there are any, can't usually be taken immediately. The quarry often moves rapidly once hit and it's necessary to re-target, which usually gives plenty of time for a manually operated rifle to be cycled. Some states limit the use of semiautomatic rifles for hunting and often severely restrict the amount of ammunition the gun can hold.

*Rapid fire in self-defense*

In reality it's hard to find examples of defensive rifle use where rapid second and third shots are strictly necessary. The rifle's inherent power and precision make it quite likely that the first accurate defensive shot will be instantly effective. Follow-up shots, if necessary, are well within the capability of both lever- and bolt-actions — assuming a practiced shooter. Again, familiarity breeds proficiency.

One not uncommon perimeter defense scenario where rapid fire may be useful is that of packs of feral predators attacking livestock. Unlike human predators, whose well-developed sense of self-preservation often causes them to break off their attack when one of their gang is shot, predatory animals often continue attacking. It may be necessary to engage more than one with accurate fire, and in such cases the semi-automatic rifle makes the task significantly easier.

A lever-action, while a little slower, can still be remarkably fast to engage those secondary targets. I personally find the bolt-action to be markedly slower, though I've met some people who could cycle the bolt as fast as I can swing a lever. They are, however, in the distinct minority — and not all bolt-actions lend themselves to such rapid manipulation. Some bolt-action rifles, such as the Steyr Scout, are built with this rapid handling capability in mind and would be preferred over those designed for the much slower pace of hunting.

## The caliber

The proper caliber for any particular shooting problem always engenders great debate, and I believe I'm vastly understating the situation! People argue endlessly about the best caliber for either self-defense or hunting, and when you combine the two, you're sure to get nothing but continuous bickering.

That being said, there are some calibers that would be sub-optimal for defensive use and are simply not allowed for most hunting. The .22 Long Rifle certainly fits into both categories (except, of course, for small game). Some, like the .223/5.56, are nearly ideal defensive calibers but not allowed for hunting in some states.*

Once you get beyond the .22-inch-diameter bullets, hunting restrictions become almost non-existent. Any 6.5mm, .30 cal, or larger diameter that would be suitable for self-defense can likely also be used for hunting. Even the Magnum pistol cartridges, such as the .357 and .44 Magnums, are eminently suitable for hunting up to 100 yards, more or less (the .357 a little less, the .44 a little more).

In states with no hunting restrictions, it's hard to argue with the .223/5.56 as an ideal utility rifle caliber. In fact, when the hunting regulations were changed in my own state, I noticed a subtle shift in the "truck guns" used by ranchers and farmers. In the past, it was common to see a .30-30 lever-action in that utility role, but today the overwhelming choice appears to be some sort of AR-15, almost always in .223/5.56.

One final thought on calibers: Because the utility rifle is intended to be a tool of wide application, it makes sense to choose a caliber with which you'll practice frequently. That means easy handling, relatively light recoil, and economy should all play parts in the caliber decision. Again, it's hard to argue with the .223/5.56, although a case could also be made for the Magnum pistol cartridges and any round in wide competition use as meeting the requirements. All of them fit the criteria better than the average heavy hunting cartridge.

## Sighting systems

When you ask the rifle to perform more tasks, the sighting system becomes more of a concern. As I noted in the chapter on sight options, anything can be pressed into service for perimeter defense, including open sights. But once you include the task of placing precise shots on game animals at longer distances, some sights become less suitable. I wouldn't want to hunt deer with open sights these days, nor even with a red-dot sight. It's hard to place bullets to a sufficient degree of precision, at distance, with either of those sights.

At the same time, magnified sights are less desirable for defensive use. This is especially true if the rifle is intended for defense inside the home, where distances are measured in feet rather than yards. The typical 3-9X hunting scope, for instance, is quite difficult to use (including set at 3X) in close quarters. It's hard to get the rifle aligned on a close target quickly with even moderately magnified optics.

### *The utility scope*

In the last few years, a type of optic has appeared on the market that is usable for both kinds of shooting. Several manufacturers now make scopes that feature a true 1X setting, which means zero apparent magnification. These scopes typically zoom up to 4X or 6X magnification for longer distances.

For years I've used fixed 4X scopes for hunting and find that magnification almost ideal for the typical distances encountered in the field. These new scopes, therefore, make nearly optimal utility optics: fast to use for defensive purposes when set at 1X, and offering more than sufficient precision when set at 4X or 6X.

For the last couple of years, I've been using such a scope, the ZD 1-4x22 RD from Meopta Sports Optics**, and have found it the perfect compromise. At 1X it's as fast as a red dot, and at 4X it's right at my preferred hunting magnification. The company also makes a 1-6X version for those who need more magnification.

Many other optic manufacturers offer these kind of scopes, usually in their "tactical" lines. Do not be fooled by the name, as they're usable over a wide range of circumstances. The important thing is to be sure that 1X is really 1X. In the past, some makers advertised scopes that were actually a little more than 1X, and even a little magnification is enough to cause usability issues at close range. It's difficult to track and engage a threat and still keep both eyes open when one of the eyes is looking at a magnified image.

In most cases, manufacturers are now labeling their scopes as being "true 1X magnification," which is what you want in a utility scope. These new optics have made the utility rifle a far more attractive and usable concept.

## The "Pool" rifle

As John Donne famously said, no man is an island. If you live in a house with other people, they may be called upon to defend themselves — or possibly you. If you're a firearms enthusiast and they're not, they may find your choice of rifle difficult to use efficiently or effectively.

For instance, if you're an avid shooter, you probably have no issue with recoil or muzzle blast. But people who aren't dedicated hobbyists often find both to be flinch-inducing. The person who picks up a rifle in an emergency, remembering the kick and blast, is likely to miss when the shot really needs to hit.

Similarly, if you're tall and have long arms but your responsible teenage daughter is shorter, the rifle sized for you may be all but unusable for her. The same goes for the operational system: A bolt-action is easy to operate quickly for someone with big hands, not so much for someone whose hands are more petite. (Having small hands for an adult male, I can personally testify to this problem.)

The solution, of course, would be for each responsible family member to have his or her own rifle tuned to their skill level and physiology. Of course for most people that's not really a solution;

aside from the cost, there are logistical issues with storage and staging.

It may be better to decide on a "pool" rifle, one designed and equipped so that every responsible household member can use it and do so well.

The pool rifle should be selected and sized for the smallest member of the household who is likely to use it. It's much easier for a large, experienced shooter to adapt to a smaller, simpler rifle than it is the opposite. If you're large and have family members who are smaller, you'll shoot much better with a smaller rifle than they will with a larger one.

Caliber should be selected to maximize hit potential rather than sheer power. Remember that the job of perimeter defense is easily accomplished with even relatively small cartridges. This is not long-range big-game hunting! A rifle in a soft-recoiling caliber, such as .223/5.56, is often a better choice for a pool rifle than one in a larger caliber.

Similarly, the operating system should be chosen for its ability to be safely and efficiently operated by the least enthusiastic person in your group. For example, many people find the semiautomatic rifle to be intimidating and confusing, no matter how many times they're taken to the range and drilled on its operation. They may find a bolt-action or lever-action rifle easier to understand and operate.

Finally, picking a gun that's fun for them to shoot increases the chances that they'll actually practice occasionally. I've found that most people love shooting the soft-recoiling M1 Carbine, and even people who profess not to like shooting often have a ball with the short, light, and friendly Carbine.

As a target or hunting rifle, the Carbine may not be anywhere near ideal, and as already mentioned, I'm not sanguine about its use in perimeter defense, but for some people under some circumstances it might be a workable solution***. That being said, the lever-action rifle chambered in .357 Magnum shares many of the handy and friendly attributes of the Carbine but offers superior performance and would be a better choice overall. It also benefits from a manual of arms many people feel is simpler than that of the semiautomatic Carbine.

Sighting systems on the pool rifle should likewise be kept simple. Don't install an optic that requires the user to remember to turn it on. Also beware of optics that require focusing. If you wear corrective lenses but your spouse doesn't, the reticle may be completely out of focus for her when she needs it in an emergency. A red dot optic, which doesn't require refocusing between users, may be a better choice.

Make it easy for everyone in your home to defend themselves and you. If that means a little rifle compromise on your part to get to that point, do so. It's better than leaving them unprotected when you're away.

---

\* - *During my research for this section, I was surprised to find how many states have changed their caliber restrictions for hunting. A decade or so ago, it was uncommon to find a state that allowed the .223/5.56 cartridge for deer hunting. Today, the situation has changed so dramatically that the states that don't allow it are now in the minority. Most states, however, prohibit the use of FMJ or "military" ammunition for hunting with those calibers and instead require expanding bullets. That shouldn't affect the use of a utility rifle because, as I pointed out in the chapter on ammunition, expanding bullets should always be your primary choice for both defense and hunting.*

\*\* - Meopta Sports Optics: www.meoptasportsoptics.com/shop/us/zd-1-4x22-rd/meotac-1-4x22-rd-true-1X-mag/ctgRus.html

\*\*\* - *If you can find one that will reliably fire a hollow-point round. Most of the commercial versions currently made seem to have great difficulty in this area.*

*Chapter Eight*
# ACCESSORIES

It has become fashionable in recent years, particularly with the ascendancy of the AR-15 pattern, to attach all manner of accessories to a rifle. It's a running joke with one of my fellow defensive shooting instructors as to what items students start removing from their rifles once they discover they're expected to carry and move around with their heavily festooned guns!

All sorts of products are on the market vying for your shooting dollar. Many of them carry the endorsement of well-known competitive shooters or people with impressive military pedigrees. Don't let either sway you: Think about the job your rifle is likely to be called upon to perform, the conditions under which it will be used, and what you need to do to get the gun to the point where it can be employed. Then select only accessories that will make the job easier or more efficient.

While I hate to crush the spirit of free enterprise and open markets, the reality is that you need precious few accessories to prepare your rifle for the job of perimeter defense. The properly trained and well-practiced shooter with an out-of-the-box Winchester .30-30 deer rifle will almost always be better prepared than the person who spent all his spare time and money accessorizing his top-of-the-line AR-15. I urge you to start with a stone-stock rifle of whatever pattern and caliber you choose, and only add accessories as you find that you really need them. Even then, think twice before hanging stuff on your rifle.

## Sights

I've covered sighting options in a separate chapter, since the topic is somewhat involved. Here I will simply caution you to approach the sighting system with careful thought.

Sights made for "close-quarters battle" may not be ideal for the job of perimeter defense at the longest plausible ranges, while those derived from long-range hunting or target shooting may be too limiting when the threat is much closer. Very few people in my classes and workshops could not do everything needed with simple open sights. That being the case, replacement or auxiliary sights should be chosen primarily to increase the range of plausible conditions under which you can employ your skills.

## Slings

Here I'm going to break from rifle orthodoxy and recommend something that is absolutely heretical. In fact, it is so antithetical to decades of rifle instruction that many simply won't consider the notion: You don't need a sling on a defensive rifle.

The sling is so much a part of historical rifle teaching that, to most people, not having one is akin to not having sights on a handgun — it's just not done! And yet the utility of a sling in perimeter defense is so limited that I feel its downsides outweigh any slight utility it may have.

The rifle sling has traditionally served a few purposes. First, it allows the comfortable carry of a rifle for long periods of time. Second, it can be used to hang the rifle in a way that permits its immediate use, much as a holster does for the handgun. Finally, used in a specific manner, the sling can enhance the shooter's long-range accuracy.

As it happens, none of those are particularly applicable to the job of perimeter defense.

The defensive rifle is the arm that needs to be retrieved from its storage space in order to be used. Most of us don't walk around with a rifle during our normal day-to-day activities. We're not on patrol like soldiers or police officers, so the need to carry it long distances doesn't exist.

Since the rifle will normally only be retrieved when it's needed, it will already be in hand and ready for use. It doesn't need to (and probably won't) be hanging in a ready-to-grab position when the time to use it comes, because it's already in your hands.

Finally, the ranges at which self-defense with a rifle is legal and ethical aren't terribly long, at least by rifle standards. The use of the sling as an aid to marksmanship isn't nearly as important as the ability to move swiftly and rapidly adopt a suitable shooting position. Any small increase in stability isn't likely to materially affect the outcome at the distances you'd expect to shoot.

So the sling isn't much of a help in the kind of incidents where you and I might be using our rifles to defend ourselves and our families. Its disadvantages, though, may make it more difficult to do that job.

One of my dislikes with the sling is that it gets in the way when you're doing anything with the rifle. When you need the rifle, you probably need it badly. It's understandable that you'll likely be shaken and anxious to get the rifle out of its storage space and to where you can use it to stop the threat. Slings tend to catch on things. If you have several rifles in the safe, and that's where you store your defensive rifle, it's not inconceivable that the sling can catch on one or more guns and take them to the floor as you're trying to get one of them into action. It's happened to me just getting a gun out for a trip to the range!

The sling makes it harder to load, manipulate, and especially transport the rifle in a hurry. As you move out of the room where the rifle is stored and go down the hallway and through other rooms and doorways, the sling will find lots of things on which it can snag. Any one of them can delay or interfere with your efficient response to a threat. I've seen this happen more than once in training scenarios and have little confidence the situation would improve when lives are on the line.

Why not, as many suggest, simply sling the rifle (put the sling over or on your body in a manner that permits the rifle's use) as you retrieve it from storage? That takes time, and in my experience (and that of the many people I've interviewed on this topic), the mind's focus will tend to be on what needs to be done *now* — and the sling isn't important to stopping the threat at the ranges we're considering.

The times when I've needed the rifle (once against another human being, the others against predatory animals on our homestead), the very last thing I thought of was "slinging up." In fact, I never thought of doing so at all — and this is consistent with what others who've been in the same kinds of emergency situations have told me.

My bottom line is simple: The sling doesn't give the home defender any actual advantage, but it does come with some observable and very real disadvantages. The return on investment just isn't there, which is why I cannot in all conscience recommend a sling for a perimeter defense rifle.

### *Bad equipment choices drive training*

It surprises me that more people don't critically examine the rifle sling. I suspect this is because most modern rifle training is based around the sling and a misguided notion of how rifles are used in private sector self-defense.

I've attended numerous classes where the shooting was always done from a "low ready" position — the rifle on the sling in front of the body, in hand, with the buttstock on or near the shoulder and the muzzle pointing down. On the fire command, the rifle is swung up, like a hinge, until it contacts the shooter's cheek, and the shooting commences.

As near as I can determine, none of that matches the way in which rifles are used in self-defense. It certainly doesn't match the manner in which I've used mine! With perimeter defense in particular, you'll be moving with the rifle to the point where you're comfortable employing (shooting) it. The rifle is unlikely to be nicely tucked into your shoulder and ready to be swung up into a perfect firing stance. Instead, you'll need to shoulder the rifle quickly from whatever position it's in when you stop running.

From a training perspective, the sling resembles the hammer in the old adage about everything looking like a nail. If the very premise of its existence isn't questioned, then it will (and does) tend to drive unrealistic training.

*For the sling holdouts*

If you can't bring yourself to abandon your sling, I strongly recommend you at least secure it in a way that minimizes its tendency to hang and snag. If you fold the sling on itself and tight against the rifle, out of the way of any operational controls, it will be much less likely to get in the way.

I've found that the elastic hair ties made to hold ponytails, referred to variously as "bobbles" or "scrunchies," are ideal for this purpose. Once the sling has been folded on itself, wrap one of the devices around the folds. This keeps it in the storage position but releases easily if you pull sharply on the sling. You may have to shop around to find a color that doesn't clash with your sling, of course.

## Ammunition carriers

At one time back in the 1990s, duplex magazine devices for the AR-15 were all the rage. These contraptions carried a spare magazine on the rifle next to the magazine well. They were usually operated by the magazine release: As the release was pushed, the spent magazine fell from the gun and the fresh magazine dropped into the shooter's hand.

The only movement necessary was to move the new magazine over an inch or so and into the magazine well. They were thought to greatly speed up magazine changes.

Well, they may or may not have done that. They certainly did cause more than one student to accidentally drop both magazines to the ground when they were put into a scenario they hadn't experienced before, when their adrenaline levels were running high and performance anxiety kicked in. I've also seen these devices jam more than one rifle, making it impossible to remove the empty magazine without opening up the receiver. They also added an uncomfortable amount of weight to the gun.

All that was bad enough, but no one ever stopped to ask if they were actually necessary.

One of the overwhelming lessons I've learned from decades of studying the use of the rifle in self-defense is that the incident is almost always solved with whatever ammunition is in the gun. Let's be realistic: We're talking about rifles, which have precision and (generally) significant force advantages over even the best handgun. Rarely do defensive rifle shootings go past the first round that accurately lands on the target.

If you've got an AR-15, for instance, you'll probably have 30 rounds in the magazine. I submit for your consideration that 30 rounds will be plenty for any fight you're ever going to have. Even the lowly bolt-action typically carries four or five rounds of high-power ammunition. Again, that's likely to be more than sufficient.

So in the harsh light of reality, is it really necessary to have spare magazine carriers attached to the rifle — or on a belt you need to remember to grab and don? Probably not.

*A rational approach to spare ammunition*

I'm not against carrying spare ammunition, as long as it's done in a manner that neither complicates the rifle nor requires you to remember to grab the ammo when you grab the gun. Thus, I concede that there are some instances where figuring out how to carry spare ammunition might be worthwhile.

If your likely perimeter defense scenario includes packs of feral predators and you're armed with the aforementioned bolt-action, you may want to have additional ammunition. This is a case of very low ammunition capacity and a large number of threats, which may require more ammunition than can be carried in the gun. In such cases, workable alternatives exist.

One popular way of carrying spare ammunition on the gun is in a buttstock band or cuff. These ammunition carriers are usually made of leather or elastic nylon and simply wrap around the buttstock. The ammunition rides on the side of the butt opposite that of your cheek when in your normal shooting position. In practice, the ammunition is pulled from the loops on the band and put into the magazine (or directly into the action of the gun) as needed. It's not fast, but given the plausibility of such a need arising, it's likely to be sufficient.

Buttstock ammunition carriers are commonly found to fit both bolt- and lever-action rifles.

There are also devices that bolt to the forearm and hold several rounds of ammunition. I've not seen any on students' guns in my classes, nor do I own one, so I can't comment on their effectiveness. I will merely make the observation that they appear to be an awkward and snag-prone approach.

Many slings have ammunition loops on them. In addition to my aversion to slings on defensive rifles, they pose another problem: If the sling is swinging around, how easy will it be to retrieve the spare ammunition?

Finally, both lever- and bolt-actions have buttstock modifications that carry spare cartridges inside the stock itself, using springs or latches to retain the rounds. I've used one rifle so equipped, and it was an elegant alternative to the buttstock cuff. But the cost is substantial, as the devices need to be installed by a qualified gunsmith to function correctly. If you have the means, this is an attractive alternative, but I can't make a blanket recommendation simply because of the cost/benefit ratio.

As you get further from the specific case of low capacity combined with multiple threats, it becomes harder to justify convoluted solutions to the perceived need for spare ammunition. For rifles with higher capacity magazines, a heavy/complex/unreliable spare ammunition device shouldn't be part of your planning. If you have a rifle with a fixed magazine of low capacity, the preceding recommendations will be more practical.

Realistically, a few rounds (or a spare magazine) in your pocket will in all likelihood see you through any scenario you might face. The problem is remembering to grab it in the stress and confusion of an actual incident.

Back to my first point: You're likely going to solve the problem with whatever ammunition is in/on the rifle. If you still feel that's not enough after a sober analysis of your own situation, it may be better to get a rifle of greater capacity than to rely on a Rube Goldberg contraption that may not work well when you need it.

**Bipods**

A bipod is a two-legged device that bolts onto the forearm of the rifle. It looks like a miniature camera tripod that's lost one of its legs — hence the term bipod. In use, the bipod's legs are swung down and out, and the rifle's forearm rests on them for a more stable prone shooting position. They're a favorite of long-range shooters, and in the last decade or so they've become common accessories found on many types of rifles.

The bipod is a device of very limited utility, as it's only useful if you're shooting from a prone position. I don't teach this shooting position in my perimeter defense courses, because it's rather unusual to find a situation where it's useful in the real world. I'll go more into this topic in the chapter on shooting positions, but suffice it to say I think the prone position is often overplayed in defensive rifle teaching.

Because the bipod is only useful from prone, it's dead weight when shooting from the more utilitarian standing, kneeling, squatting, and sitting positions. The weight is also well forward on the gun, which makes it harder to handle and more tiring to hold or carry. The bipod's legs usually face forward when stowed, making them likely to snag on just about anything in the environment.

Finally, a good bipod is expensive — money that, for a defensive rifle, can be better spent on more useful things, like ammunition and training.

As a long-range shooting aid, particularly in a competition environment, the bipod has a lot to recommend it. As a hunting tool, it's less valuable (and adds weight that has to be carried all day). In a defensive context, it's nearly useless.

## Grips

The advent of the AR-15 as the nation's most popular sporting and defensive rifle has resulted in a wide range of accessories becoming available. Some of them, such as grips, were never a possibility when rifle stocks were made of wood or fiberglass and carved to shape in the gun factory.

Pistol grips for the AR-15 come in a bewildering variety of shapes, sizes, textures, and materials. I've not found any of them to sufficiently improve my shooting ability with the rifle except in very odd extreme circumstances (such as forcing myself to shoot with one hand).

That being said, you may find a specific grip makes your rifle more comfortable or gives you more confidence in your ability to manipulate the trigger. If so, by all means use it! The rifle you're more comfortable with is the one you'll practice with, and the more practice you get in, the better.

My only warning is to avoid grips with any sort of finger grooves. The standard AR-15 A2 grip, the one that comes on most entry-level guns, doesn't fit anyone's hand well. In my case, it makes getting a good high hand position — necessary for a straight manipulation of the trigger — nearly impossible. This is true of most grips that force your hand into a specific position. I recommend a plain grip, one in which you can "choke up" as high as necessary without causing your hand any discomfort.

Many grips are on the market, and you should have no trouble finding something suitable. Grips for the AR-15 (and similar rifles) are cheap, widely available, and easily changed. There's very little downside to installing one that makes your shooting time more pleasant.

*Foregrips*

The same accessory market that has brought us better shooting-hand grips for the AR-15 has also brought us a number of forearm grips for the support hand. These foregrips, as they're known, are purported to make the rifle easier to use in rapid fire or to make transitioning between targets faster. In my personal experience, their utility is significantly less clear.

The interesting thing about the rifle is that your relationship to the gun changes with small changes in your shooting position. Shooting from a squatting position, for example, puts your torso at a different angle to the axis of the barrel than, say, a standing position. (This is partly due to your natural point of aim being more restricted in a crouch than when upright. I'll cover this more in the chapter on shooting positions.) As a result, your support hand ends up in different positions on the rifle as your shooting stance changes, making a fixed foregrip sub-optimal at least part of the time, and possibly even unusable.

Many foregrips, particularly those that protrude at right angles from the barrel, are quite good at providing a handy protrusion on which you can snag the gun as you move through the environment. This can be reduced substantially by moving the foregrip closer to the shooting handgrip, but on an AR-15, this usually results in the foregrip being just in front of the magazine well. In that case, it's easier, faster, cheaper, and lighter to just use the magazine well as the foregrip, which is something I do frequently.

For these reasons, I don't generally recommend foregrips on defensive rifles. I'd much rather have the versatility and adaptability of being able to place my support arm anywhere on the forearm that it needs to be — or feels best being. The major exception to my opinion concerns rifles with very short barrels, such as bullpups or SBRs*, where there isn't much (if any) forearm to grasp. In those cases, a foregrip may be the only way to effectively support the front of the rifle.

The ultimate abomination is a foregrip on a bolt-action rifle. The bolt-action doesn't have an issue with muzzle rise during rapid fire, which is one of the few arguments for a foregrip, and with one the support hand ends up with less control over the gun as the bolt is cycled by the shooting hand. Very rarely one such equipped rifle shows up in class and, after some realistic shooting exercises, the owners almost invariably remove them. (The same is often true for AR-15 owners.)

Accessorize only when it makes sense to do so, and choose your accessories carefully.

---

*\* - "SBR" is a legal term meaning "short barreled rifle," the federal definition of a rifle whose barrel is shorter than 16 inches. Such rifles must be registered with the Bureau of Alcohol, Tobacco, Firearms & Explosives (BATFE), and a $200 tax paid.*

## Chapter Nine
# AMMUNITION

If you're forced to fire your rifle against an intruder, whether the threat is human or animal, your goal is always to stop the threat as quickly as possible. It's to your advantage to use ammunition that does so as efficiently as possible, to both rapidly eliminate the threat and reduce the dangers of collateral damage or casualties. The fewer rounds you expend, the better for you, those around you, and — ironically — the attacker.

At the same time, you also need ammunition for practice and training with your rifle, because the ammo you use to defend yourself may be too expensive for regular use. For this reason, you also need training/practice ammo that matches the handling characteristics of your defensive loads.

**Defensive ammunition**

Defensive ammunition for the rifle should always contain an expanding projectile (bullet). Expanding bullets increase their frontal diameter as they contact and move through the target, making larger wound tracks and increasing the relative lethality of the round. Hunters have long known the value of expanding bullets, and you won't find many hunting bullets that aren't designed to expand inside game*.

Expanding rifle bullets usually come in two main styles: soft-point and hollow-point.

*Soft-points*

The soft-point bullet is made of lead with a tough copper jacket that stops short of the bullet's tip, leaving the soft lead exposed. When the soft tip contacts the target, the lead deforms and splits the jacket, allowing the rest of the bullet to flatten out to a larger diameter. The degree and rapidity of that expansion are controlled by varying the jacket thickness (and sometimes the internal construction of the bullet). The soft-point is the most common rifle bullet design and has a long history of success.

The downside of the soft-point bullet is that the soft lead tip is easily damaged by rough handling. This can affect the accuracy of the round and also alter its expansion characteristics. The tips can also be damaged by feeding through a semiautomatic rifle action, while the soft lead can also drag on the feed ramps of such rifles and result in unreliable feeding.

To get around these problems, some manufacturers substitute a polymer tip for the exposed lead. The polymer is less susceptible to permanent deformation and can be made to be more aerodynamic for better accuracy and range. The expansion mechanism remains similar to that of the traditional soft-point.

*Hollow-points*

In the hollow-point bullet design, the soft lead projectile has a cavity or dimple on the top of the copper-jacketed bullet. When the hollow-point contacts a fleshy target, fluid in the target collects inside the hollow-point cavity. Since water, which accounts for the majority of fluid in a living entity, is non-compressible, the forward motion of the bullet causes intense pressure to build inside the cavity. That pressure causes the cavity to open outward, increasing the bullet's effective diameter. This deformation continues down the bullet, and like the soft-point, is controlled by the design and thickness of the jacket.

Hollow-point rounds are available in a wide range of calibers but are more common with larger-caliber and/or slower cartridges. Depending on the design, the hollow-point has the capability for violent expansion at relatively low velocities. This is why they are the preferred design for defensive handgun rounds. The much higher velocities encountered in rifle rounds tend to result in excessive expansion with hollow-points, resulting in fragmentation and shallow wound tracks.

In recent years, some makers have designed and produced all-copper hollow-point bullets, combining the hollow-point with a much tougher bullet material to limit expansion. Such bullets perform very much like soft-point designs and have many adherents.

For defensive purposes, you want an expanding bullet of some sort. I've found that bullets designed specifically to take down light-skinned large game, such as deer, make almost ideal perimeter defense rounds. They have suitable power, range, accuracy, and expansion characteristics to be usable over a wide range of plausible threats.

**Practice ammunition**

Soft-point or hollow-point ammunition is difficult to manufacture compared to non-expanding (often referred to as "ball" ammunition) types. As a result, it is more expensive. This doesn't matter to the average hunter, who fires only a few rounds to perhaps a box of ammunition per year. Using your rifle in defense of yourself, your family, or your homestead requires more skill. You need to be able to reliably hit a variety of targets at ranges from very close to perhaps the limits of your property line — and you must do it under the extreme stress of an attack, perhaps in low light, and still be able to make decisions while you shoot.

The only way to develop and maintain these specialized shooting skills is to practice frequently and realistically — in other words, similar to how you'll expect to react during an attack. This requires the expenditure of ammunition, and the responsible defensive shooter expends hundreds of rounds per year in training and practice. Unless you're quite well off, shooting defensive ammunition quickly eats into your preparedness budget!

For this reason, you need good practice ammunition that matches the handling characteristics of your defensive ammunition. Look for the same bullet weight, in a shape as close to your defensive rounds as possible. Such ammunition should have similar recoil and point-of-impact properties to your defensive rounds, making it unnecessary to figure in allowances for the different bullets.

Look for full metal jacket (FMJ) rounds in the same weight as your defensive ammunition. FMJ is the cheapest bullet to make, and many cartridges are made with your choice of FMJ or an expanding bullet. Some cartridges, however, don't have that choice. In such cases, find the cheapest variety of ammunition you can that has the same bullet weight and use it for your practice.

**Loading your own ammunition**

Rifle ammunition of all types is much more expensive than handgun ammunition. The pricing differential between handloaded and store-bought ammo is much higher for rifles than for pistols and revolvers, making "home-rolled" ammunition more attractive.

I'm an accomplished handloader myself, and I know how much more I can shoot by making my own ammunition. I do in fact produce much of my own practice ammo. It's very easy to buy inexpensive bullets and craft a load that precisely matches my defensive ammunition.

But when it comes to the ammunition I expect to use against an actual threat, I always load factory ammo. The first reason is reliability. I've met many people who claim to produce ammunition in their basement that is "more reliable" than what they can get from a major ammunition manufacturer, but I have yet to find anyone who could actually demonstrate that they did (this includes my own ammunition). I'd rather trust my well-being to ammunition produced through modern quality control than even my anal-retentive loading habits.

Most importantly, though, is the possibility of forensic testing after a shooting against a human attacker. Should such testing become a point in a shooting investigation, exemplar ammunition with lot numbers that match the rounds used may be needed for testing. Rounds from an independent ammunition maker who understands the concept of "chain of evidence" is more likely to be admitted into court than my reloading records.

In a case where the validity of a defensive shooting may come into question, I want all the advantages on my side. Using factory ammunition gives me one less thing to worry about.

Keep in mind that your defensive rounds may never be used, or if they are, you'll only use a few a year. Even in my area, where defense against predators is fairly common, I might shoot an average of two or three rounds in an entire year. At that rate, even the most expensive factory ammunition isn't a major expense! I've crafted inexpensive practice loads that duplicate factory performance, so I can practice cheaply then load up with the ammunition designed to give me every advantage — both when I pull the trigger, and when the justice system looks with a jaundiced eye at what I did.

Handloaders can get the best of both worlds: reliable and effective factory ammunition for defense, and cheap matching rounds for extensive practice. I can't think of a more compelling argument for learning to reload your own ammunition.

### Recommendations by caliber

When we talk about perimeter defense, we're considering engagements from just beyond what is normally considered handgun distance (say, 15 yards) to the extent of a legally defensible property line (up to perhaps 100 yards or so, depending on the nature of the threat). The reality is that just about any expanding bullet out of a rifle will probably work very well. As a result, your exact ammunition choice won't be critical, but there are some exceptions.

Remember that you don't need super deep penetrating bullets capable of taking down huge animals. What you need is a bullet that will expand on relatively thin-skinned game at moderate distances. At the same time, the bullet needs to resist the kind of fragmentation that reduces effectiveness. The very delicate bullets for small game or varmint shooting, for instance, may not reliably incapacitate an attacker — whether animal or human — at typical perimeter defense distances.

This listing is not exhaustive and isn't intended to be. These are the cartridges that are commonly found and with which I have actual shooting experience. Many other cartridges would be perfectly suitable for the task of perimeter defense, but by studying these recommendations — focusing on my explanations — you should be able to easily extrapolate what would work well for your favorite rifle round.

*.223 Remington/5.56x45mm:*** The .223, chambered in the ubiquitous AR-15 pattern rifle, is in wide service with our military and law enforcement. It's also the most popular centerfire rifle chambering in the civilian world and shows no evidence of giving up that title anytime soon.

At the defensive distances we're considering in the private sector, most expanding bullets in this caliber will work fairly well. That being said, I prefer to stay in the range of 55 to 62 grains. First, because they're by far the most common and are loaded by all the major makers. Second, it's easy to find cheap practice ammunition in those weights, which is not the case with the heavier or lighter projectiles. Third, they stabilize properly in all barrel twists. And last, they shoot to point of aim within the adjustment capabilities of all iron sights, scopes, and red-dot sights.

This is a cartridge that is commonly loaded with lighter bullets designed for rapid expansion and sold for varmint hunting. This is why

I recommend going no lighter than 55 grains, which are generally designed and sold for medium game. Those bullets will both expand and penetrate well.

Various loads in this caliber are designed and sold specifically for law enforcement use. I don't recommend those, as their performance tends to be weighted toward glass and auto door penetration. They may not perform as well as a "lesser" bullet against someone who's not hiding in a car.

My favorite .223/5.56 defensive factory load is the 55-grain Hornady Spire Point, a traditional lead-point bullet that has shown good performance on the animals I've shot. I believe I can trust it to hold together while still expanding inside the target. Similar rounds are made by all the major manufacturers, and I would have no hesitation picking up any of them to use in any .223 rifle. I recommend choosing a similar bullet in either 55 or 62 grain and then buying several boxes of the same-weight Full Metal Jacket (FMJ) ammunition for cheap practice.

If you are an enthusiast, a handloader, and understand the specifics of the rifling twist in your gun, you may choose to go to one of the heavy 75- to 77-grain loads. These have proven quite effective at longer ranges on tough game such as wild hogs and would be ideal as a perimeter defense round. The only issue is stabilization: The 77-grain bullets, in particular, require a minimum of a 1:8 twist to maintain accuracy — and some barrels so marked are a little "slow" and still won't work well with the heavy bullets. If you have a 1:7 barrel, you'll be fine, but that's an uncommon twist for AR-15 rifles these days.

***.30 Carbine:*** The lowly .30 Carbine developed something of a checkered reputation in World War II, but it's a round that penetrates very deeply with the smooth, round-nosed jacketed bullet typically loaded in the cartridge. Those streamlined bullets tend to go through a target without much tissue disruption as compared to higher-speed rifle rounds. However, adding an expanding bullet to the Carbine makes it into a formidable defensive round. I've talked to police officers who've used such loads against criminals, and the results were more than satisfactory. My own experience shooting medium-sized animals with the .30 Carbine tallies with their conclusions.

The Carbine's major limitation is range. At the most extreme distances that we'll consider to be perimeter defense, the little Carbine starts to run low on power. This shouldn't dissuade you if you have a Carbine and like its combination of fast handling and light recoil, but understand that those 75- or 100-yard shots must be carefully considered and aimed to be reliably effective.

As I hinted, the full metal jacket (FMJ) or military ball rounds commonly found for the .30 Carbine are not at all recommended. But as this is written, alternatives are scarce. Winchester is the only major company currently loading a hollow-point*** in the .30 Carbine; it's a 110-grain bullet that, in my experience, performs quite well. The big issue is that not every Carbine feeds this load well, as the little guns are well known for being particular about ammunition. The post-war reproductions from various companies have especially spotty reliability with defensive ammunition.

You need to test your Carbine thoroughly with your chosen defensive ammunition before relying on it for defensive purposes. If it won't shoot the load reliably, I urge you to use (or acquire, if necessary) a different gun to protect yourself and your family.

*.30-30 Winchester:* At first glance, this old deer hunter's favorite may seem an odd inclusion, but I've been following defensive shooting stories for a couple of decades, and this is a commonly used round against intruders both inside and outside the home.

One reason, I suspect, is because of the lever-action rifle's ubiquity in American homes. Light, trim rifles were designed to be quick to shoulder and swing on target, and their relatively mild recoil compared to more powerful rifles makes them friendlier to shoot. It's not surprising, then, that this familiar and reliable rifle — and the .30-30 round most closely associated with it — might be the first gun that's grabbed in an emergency.

Whatever the explanation, I see a lot of defensive shootings with the old "thutty-thutty." This round has a long track record in hunting use, and it's easy to find a load that will work against the kind of threats we find in perimeter defense.

So well developed is this cartridge that just about any 150-grain softpoint bullet from any established ammunition maker will give good service — and can double as an effective hunting round during deer season. If you want a personal recommendation, my preferred defensive round in the .30-30 is the Winchester 150-grain Jacketed Hollow Point (JHP). I have decades of experience with this load, and its renowned performance in game also makes it ideal for perimeter defense. It displays good penetration and excellent expansion at all reasonable distances.

A second choice, and the only ammunition from a non-major maker I'll recommend, is the Barnes 150-grain VOR-TX load. Barnes is a well-established bullet and hunting ammunition manufacturer. Though not known for defensive ammunition, their rifle bullets perform excellently under the conditions we're considering.

*.357 Magnum:* What's the .357 Magnum doing in a book about defensive rifles? Well, the Magnum is chambered in light, handy lever-action rifles from a variety of manufacturers. It's also a round whose performance completely changes when fired from a barrel longer than that of a typical revolver.

I've often said that the .357 is a schizophrenic round, because it has two distinct personalities depending on what gun it's fired from. The .357 gains a huge performance boost out of a rifle barrel — as much as 500 feet-per-second faster than out of a revolver. This changes the performance of the bullet dramatically and puts it into the performance envelope of some .30-30 loads at short distances.

Even with all that increased performance, recoil and muzzle blast are very mild as far as rifles go. It's easily handled by shooters of all sizes and experience levels, which makes it an ideal "pool" gun for the whole family to use.

I've shot .357 rifles quite a bit at various sizes of game and have come away with a pretty good idea of just how the cartridge performs when fired from a rifle. As it happens, ammunition made for the Magnum generally assumes modest revolver velocities, and many bullets just disintegrate on impact when shot from a rifle. This leads to shallow wounds that don't reliably incapacitate the target.

As a result, I recommend staying with heavier bullets noted for their tougher construction. I've found the Hornady 158-grain XTP load to be excellent from a rifle barrel, with good expansion and penetration without coming apart. My second choice is the Winchester 158-grain Jacketed Soft Point, but I avoid the Remington and Federal versions of this load. In my experience, they don't hold together at rifle velocities as well as the Winchesters.

The .357 Magnum rifle is effective out to the limits of what can be considered self-defense against either human or animal predators. In my house, it's typically the first gun I grab when a problem presents itself.

*.308 Winchester:* This round is the "jack of all trades" cartridge. It's been used for everything from varmint to big-game hunting, from military sniping to long-range competition, and just about everything in between. The .308 is chambered in bolt-, lever-, and semiautomatic actions and, while it's not necessarily the absolute best at any given job, it's usually more than sufficiently capable. It's also chambered in one of the more popular rifles sold today, the AR-10 pattern.

The .308 has more than enough power and range to be instantly effective at the job of perimeter defense. In fact, it may sometimes be a little too powerful and the bullets it fires a little too tough to expand reliably on thin-skinned targets. Loads for the .308 must therefore be carefully chosen — then again, it's the variety of loads available that makes this round so versatile!

For the tasks we'll consider in this book, I recommend a soft-point bullet in the 125-grain range, which is loaded by several manufacturers and readily available. You might also consider a rapidly expanding varmint-type bullet in the 150-grain weight range if you anticipate shots on dangerous feral or rabid animals at the outer limits of what we're considering (around 100 yards).

**Want more ammunition information?**

A more thorough discussion of defensive ammunition and how it works can be found in my *free* ebook, *How To Choose Self Defense Ammunition*. Download your free copy at this link:

www.getgrant.us/PYH

---

\* - *The exceptions are bullets designed for very large, heavy, dangerous game animals where penetration is needed above all else. In those cases, large diameter (caliber) cartridges are chosen along with solid, non-expanding projectiles. Unless you live in the depths of Africa, where attacks by hippos or Cape Buffalo are common, this should not prove to be a concern.*

\*\* - *These two rounds are commonly interchanged, but that's not an entirely safe practice. This is a very good article about the differences and when they're important:*

*http://www.luckygunner.com/labs/5-56-vs-223/*

\*\*\* - *Federal and Remington load a jacketed soft point in the Carbine, but my experience with them suggests they are much inferior to the hollowpoint bullet loaded by Winchester.*

*Chapter Ten*

# STORING AND RETRIEVING YOUR RIFLE

The defensive rifle differs from the defensive handgun in power, range, and precision. That much you already know. But another difference greatly affects how and what you train: the need to retrieve the rifle.

The defining characteristic of perimeter defense is the need to retrieve the rifle from where it's being stored and transport it to the point where it can be used against the threat.

The defensive handgun is the tool you can carry discreetly on your person. Aside from wardrobe and legality considerations, the handgun is the weapon you can have with you all the time, the tool that is always ready and at hand should you need it. As a result, the doctrine of use and the training for that doctrine have evolved to recognize and take advantage of that constant availability.

The rifle, on the other hand, isn't usually being carried. Unless you're out hunting or assigned to a military or law enforcement patrol, the rifle isn't going to be readily at hand. It's the defensive tool you must retrieve in order to use. You have to go to where the rifle is stored, get it out of its storage place or space, and carry it to the point where you can employ it.

It doesn't sound terribly complicated, does it? In practice, though, it turns out to greatly affect your training, and the first thing you need to do is train yourself to abandon your position to get your rifle.

**The fire extinguisher story**

Have you ever been faced with a sudden fire? It might be a bonfire that gets out of control, a barbeque that ignites the dry grass around it, an engine that erupts in flames on the highway, or perhaps an electrical short or grease fire. My first experience was a tractor that set off a field fire.

If you've ever experienced an unexpected or out-of-control fire, you know the panic it causes.

The curious thing about fire is that you know you need tools, such as a water hose or extinguisher, to fight it, but there is a strong pull to stay and attempt to fight the fire without tools anyhow. You know you need an extinguisher to keep the fire from growing, but you're so busy stomping the ground or using your coat to keep the flames at bay that you feel you just don't have time to go get the extinguisher that will put out the fire for good.

It's an odd feeling, knowing what you need to do but believing you can't do it because in the interim, the situation will get worse. If you just stay there, you think, it won't get any worse. I've experienced that feeling more than once, and it causes a great deal of panic.

The first thing you need to do is break away from the incident to reach the tool you need to deal with it most efficiently. In perimeter defense, that tool is the rifle — and it's not likely to be convenient to get to.

Because of the natural feelings of panic you'll probably experience, everything will seem to move slowly and every little impediment you encounter will seem greater than it really is. Any slight delay will feel like an eternity, and you'll no doubt fumble around a bit as you try to lay your hands on your rifle.

## Staging for successful retrieval

As you move the rifle from the storage place to where you'll actually use it, you'll no doubt have to maneuver around objects (perhaps even people) and through doorways and gates. Each time you encounter one of those obstacles, any handling difficulties will be magnified in your mind, making the panic worse.

When you need your rifle, you're likely to be in a great hurry and already under the effects of panic. You certainly don't need any more delays, and planning ahead to eliminate them will help make your response more efficient.

By properly staging the rifle — storing it in a manner and place that make it easier to retrieve — you can significantly reduce delays and make your response more efficient.

### *Staging safely and securely*

As mentioned in the safety chapter, it's your responsibility to store your firearm so it can't be accessed or used by unauthorized people. That means children, visitors, friends, house cleaners, and especially thieves.

The best solution is to keep it in a locked safe. The problem with the traditional rifle safe is that it's difficult to access in a hurry. The dial combination lock isn't fast under any conditions, and when panic sets in, it becomes even more difficult to operate.

Most dial locks have a key over-ride, which is a little better in terms of sheer speed, but you have to remember to always have the key with you. It's also fumble-prone. Ever tried to insert a key in a lock upside-down when you're in a hurry?

Many rifle safes are available with a keypad electronic lock. These are substantially easier to operate when in a hurry than the old dial type. Many people question their security and longevity versus the mechanical dial lock, but if you buy your safe from a reputable safe manufacturer, you shouldn't have issues. Most of my friends long ago switched to the electronic locks, and none have reported any issues.

The best way to securely stage a perimeter defense rifle and still get to it quickly in an emergency is with a quick-access lockbox designed for long guns. (I intentionally use the word "lockbox" instead of "safe" because lockboxes aren't burglar-resistant and shouldn't be thought of as theft protection.)

These are usually sized to hold one rifle or shotgun, and typically mount to the floor under a bed or sofa. A few models will bolt to a wall, somewhat like a surface-mounted medicine cabinet, and others are sold to be mounted into a vehicle. All work for staging your defensive rifle.

Many quick-access lockboxes use some form of biometric lock (fingerprint reader). I'm not yet sold on these devices, as I've tested them with slightly dirty and/or sweaty fingers and they often fail to read. They work wonderfully if your fingers are clean and dry, but what if you're gardening on a hot day and suddenly need your rifle?

For this reason, I prefer quick-access lockboxes that use a push-button lock, either electronic or mechanical. Those that use a pattern lock, with five buttons that are pushed in a specific sequence to unlock, are probably the best compromise between speed and security. My second choice is a conventional electronic lock with a full numbered keypad.

I want to reiterate that these lockboxes are not intended to be burglar-resistant — and they aren't. They're designed for secure storage of a ready-to-use defensive firearm that needs to be kept away from unauthorized users. Anyone with even rudimentary tools, such as a screwdriver, can very easily defeat their minimal protection and steal your rifle.

If you leave your house unattended, I highly recommend transferring your rifle from the quick-access lockbox and into a traditional and more secure gun safe.

*Where to stage*

Deciding where to stage your defensive rifle is a matter of balancing conflicting needs. Keeping it under the bed or in a bedroom closet is very handy should you need to retrieve it during the night. For home defense (inside the home), that may be ideal. If you need the rifle during the day, though, the bedroom may not be the best choice.

Since most bedrooms, particularly master bedrooms, are positioned in the back of the house, you may have to maneuver through a room or two, a hallway, and at least a couple of doorways to get to your rifle. That's a long trek during an emergency!

Another choice is to mount the quick-access lockbox under a sofa in a living or family room. These rooms are generally centralized in the home, making them readily accessible from both inside and outside. The downside to this location is that, if you plan to use your rifle for defense inside the home, it may not be safe to try to gain access during an attack where intruders have made it inside. If that's the location you choose, you'll also need to plan for a defensive firearm you can access quickly in your bedroom.

Staging your perimeter defense rifle in a lockbox in a secondary bedroom, den, or office is another choice. These are usually closer to the center of the house than the master bedroom and are consequently easier to access quickly. The downside is the same as staging in the living room: If you need the rifle for defense inside the home you may not be able to get to it without exposing yourself to an intruder. You'll still need to keep a defensive firearm in your bedroom where you can access it easily and quickly.

As you can see, there are tradeoffs to every staging location. No book can possibly cover all the variations in home design and decor that affect your choice. I suggest you look at your house layout with a critical eye, thinking of the circumstances under which you would likely need a defensive rifle and how easy it would be to access it in an emergency — including from outside the house.

*How to stage*

Ideally, your defensive rifle would be staged in a single-gun lockbox. All you need to do in that case is open the box and grab the rifle. I recognize, however, that this might not be the solution you choose for your specific circumstances. You may decide to keep your perimeter defense rifle in a safe with other guns, but that decision comes with some issues.

*Here's a big reason why I don't recommend a sling:* Back in the chapter on accessories, I explained my dislike of slings on defensive rifles. I don't know about you, but any time I take a rifle out of a safe (which is its most likely storage space), the sling always seems to catch on any and all other rifles or shotguns that are in there. No matter how carefully I stack things, the sling on the rifle I want snags on something else. I end up having to disentangle things just to get the gun I want.

Now apply the lesson from the fire extinguisher story: When an incident happens and you run to grab your perimeter defense rifle only to find the sling hanging up, it's not likely to be a calming moment. You might spill other long guns onto the floor, exacerbating the situation and requiring you to untangle the mess. From experience, I can say it will seem like an eternity. The situation will be made worse by fumbling to extricate the rifle and being delayed even further by the fumbling.

Getting rid of the sling, which isn't going to have much utility in the context of self-defense, is a good way to avoid a potential problem.

*Orientation while staged:* Think about how you'll be putting your hands on the rifle when the safe or lockbox is opened. Are you right- or left-handed? Which direction does the door open? Which direction will you need to turn to exit the area? All of these factor into your decision on storing your rifle.

You shouldn't need to change hands while retrieving the rifle. For instance, I'm right-handed and my safe's hinges are on the left side. It's against a wall, so the safe door doesn't quite open all the way. If I'm using an AR-15 as my defensive rifle and it's sitting on the left side of the safe, muzzle up and the pistol grip pointing to the left, I can't easily get my left hand onto the forearm to retrieve the rifle.

I also can't grab the pistol grip with my right hand and lift the rifle out, because I'd have little to no control over the direction of the muzzle. I'm limited to grabbing the forearm with my right hand. The issue with doing so is that I'd need to swap hands — my left hand would need to be on the forearm and my right hand would need to go to the pistol grip, which means a bit of fumbling to get my hands to where they need to be.

It would be better to store the gun on the right side of the safe with the pistol grip pointing to the right, so my right hand can easily grasp where it will actually be when using the gun. However, the muzzle pointing up isn't stable until the rifle is lifted to the point that its center of mass is over my right hand. The muzzle will wobble a bit, perhaps unsafely, while I lift the rifle out of the safe.

The best solution in my case is to store the rifle toward the right side of my safe, where my right hand can get to it easily even before the safe door is fully opened. The rifle would be stored muzzle down and the pistol grip pointed at the door of the safe. This way, I can reach in with my hand in a natural position, getting onto the grip in a position very close to what it would be if I were shooting. As I lift the rifle from the safe, the center of mass is below my hand, and gravity helps stabilize the rifle. The muzzle will automatically be pointed in a safe direction (I live in a one-level home), and I'll be able to maneuver safely and quickly.

Think through how you store your rifle and what physical manipulations you need to make in order to retrieve your rifle. Using an unloaded gun, experiment with different placements and figure out which will be best for you.

Remember you'll likely be retrieving your rifle in a state of at least mild panic. Factor in the mind's normal desire to short-cut the procedure because you're in a hurry. Stage your rifle so you have the most control and the least amount of hand switching after contact.

**Loaded or not?**

One topic of debate is whether the defensive rifle should be stored loaded or unloaded. Many people liken it to the handgun you carry, and they insist that, like the handgun, your rifle should be immediately ready to use.

There is a flaw with this line of thinking. The concealed carry handgun is a tool you carry to address a sudden need — a surprise attack of which you had little to no foreknowledge. The attack occurs when you don't expect it and presents an immediate threat. Because of the attack's sudden and surprising nature, you might not have both hands available. The handgun needs to be ready to use immediately and with a minimum of manipulation, because you don't have time to do anything else. It is therefore normally carried loaded and ready to fire, as it should be.

The rifle, on the other hand, is the defensive tool you need to go and get. It takes time to access. It has to be retrieved and brought to the point where it can be used, which makes it a more deliberate tool. You take the time to access the rifle because you need (or have decided you need) its unique combination of precision, power, and range.

The rifle is the tool you use because you've decided you need its capabilities, not because it's convenient.

Keeping the staged rifle in a loaded and ready-to-fire condition isn't as important as keeping the defensive handgun in that condition. If you have enough time to retrieve your rifle, you have enough time to load it.

Storing the rifle unloaded is safer in general, and may be better for the longevity of the springs in the gun.

At the same time, there is no reason to make the loading any slower or more difficult than it needs to be. A rifle using a detachable magazine, such as the AR-15, is relatively easy to load — you just insert the magazine into the gun. But if your defensive rifle is a lever-action, loading is a more involved, dexterity-intensive, and time-consuming process.

*The ready compromise*

To balance safety with ease of use, I suggest storing your perimeter defense rifle in what's known as "cruiser ready" condition. This is a term from the world of law enforcement, from back in the days when they carried a shotgun in their patrol vehicle, up front in a dash holder next to their radio. The shotgun was stored with the safety on and the magazine tube fully loaded, but no shell in the chamber. This made the gun nearly as safe as one that was completely unloaded, but it could be easily brought into firing condition by pumping a shell into the chamber and thumbing off the safety.

Cruiser ready makes a lot of sense for a staged defensive rifle. If you should you need the rifle, it's a quick matter to chamber a round as part of your retrieval routine. You lose nothing in practical speed of access, but the rifle is in a substantially safer condition for storage and handling.

*Putting the rifle into cruiser-ready condition*

If your rifle has a safety, make sure it's in the on or safe position. Pointing the rifle in a known safe direction*, open the chamber; if your rifle is a semiautomatic, lock the bolt open. Double-check that the chamber is empty, then check it again. Carefully close the bolt on the verified empty chamber.

If you're using a bolt-action rifle with a detachable magazine, depress the trigger while closing the bolt. This will safely un-tension the firing pin into a relaxed, rather than cocked, state.**

If you're using a lever-action rifle with an exposed hammer, close the lever, put your thumb on the hammer to restrain it, and then depress the trigger. Slowly lower the hammer until it is in the rest position.

For all other rifles, close the action. Keeping the rifle pointed in a safe direction, take the safety off and pull the trigger to dry-fire the gun. Once that's done, re-engage the safety if it's possible to do so. (The AR-15 family of rifles will not allow you to put the gun on safe if the hammer is not cocked.)

You now have a rifle with an empty chamber and any hammer or firing-pin springs in a relaxed state. The rifle can be safely stored for very long periods of time in this condition without worrying about the springs taking a set or otherwise being weakened.

You may now load the rifle's magazine. For lever-action rifles with tubular magazines, load the magazine through the loading port. Some lever-actions have a loading port on the side of the receiver, while others require loading through a port near the end of the magazine.

For bolt-action rifles with non-detachable magazines, open the floorplate. Holding the rifle upside down, drop the ammunition into the open magazine — making sure they're oriented in the correct direction. Close and latch the floorplate.

For rifles with detachable magazines, load a magazine and insert it firmly into the rifle until it latches in place. In some cases, fully loaded magazines may be very difficult (if not impossible) to insert on a closed bolt. The 30-round AR-15 magazine is a perfect example: The strong tension of the magazine spring when loaded doesn't have enough give to allow the rounds to move downward when pressed against the closed bolt. In these cases, taking a round or two out of the magazine generally allows it to be seated in the rifle.

It's usually a good practice to give the bottom of the magazine a strong rap with the heel of your hand in order to firmly seat it in the gun, then tug the magazine to ensure that it is latched securely. Some rifles will not reliably retain the magazine if this isn't done.

### From storage to employment

As I mentioned earlier, the rifle is the defensive arm that must be retrieved and taken from the point where it is staged to the point where it can be used. If the rifle is being used inside the home for protection against an intruder, that distance may be a few feet.

But in perimeter defense, that distance is likely to be measured in yards and entail maneuvering around and through things. The place you use the rifle is likely to be outside the confines of your house, even if it's just a step outside the door. This places many more demands on how you handle the rifle, particularly when you need to maneuver around other people.

*When do you chamber a round?*

Many people recommend you chamber a round, readying the rifle for use, as you retrieve it from storage. The rationale is that the rifle needs to be ready immediately should you be set upon by an attacker.

I agree with the sentiment, but it needs to be tempered with some practicality. Taking the time to calmly chamber a round before you run for the door is tough, and the temptation is to grab the rifle and chamber a round while you're already moving. That's an incredibly dangerous practice, and in the heat of the moment, you might not even realize you're doing it.

The very nature of perimeter defense requires you to move with a rifle, and moving with a loaded rifle increases the risk rather substantially.

A secondary component of that same rush to get back to the incident is a possible failure to engage the safety once the ammunition is in the chamber. Having a loaded, chambered rifle whose safety is not engaged — while under stress — is a disaster in the making.

I've seen both happen in classes where I've put students under a bit of stress as part of a shooting exercise, and I've seen them in a competition environment as well. The desire to get a better score, to get through the exercise faster than peers or other competitors, can lead to taking shortcuts. If it happens in a controlled environment, I submit that it's more likely to happen in an uncontrolled one.

Then there are rifles like the AR-15 that can't be chambered with the safety firmly set in the on position. The safety has to be applied after the round is chambered, which means you need to remember to do so. Moving around quickly with a loaded, off-safe rifle while in an understandably agitated state is a recipe for an accident. Accidents with loaded rifles often have tragic outcomes.

Because you'll be moving from one enclosed point (where the rifle is stored) to an open point (likely outside, where the rifle needs to be employed), the loaded and chambered rifle presents a whole host of safety concerns. While with enough training and practice, it's possible to do it safely, it's not something that comes naturally. Erring on the side of caution under such circumstances by having a gun that is loaded but not chambered adds a layer of safety to an already chaotic incident.

For these reasons, I recommend chambering a round when you get to the point of employment\*\*\*. If your gun safe is in your bedroom and you're going to be using the rifle in the bedroom against an attacker, you can chamber a round immediately. But if you've run into your bedroom to retrieve the rifle because of a threat in your yard, the place of employment will be somewhere outside of your door. Chamber a round when you get there.

This is contrary to how most hunters, who are worried about scaring their quarry by noisily chambering a round, operate. The same is true for military personnel, who worry that the sound of the bolt opening and closing will give away their position to the enemy. In self-defense, this isn't a concern, as it's unlikely that your attacker, whether human or animal, doesn't already know you're there.

It's also contrary to the practice and recommendation for the defensive handgun. But a valid reason exists for treating them differently.

You carry a concealed handgun to deal with a surprise threat that requires an immediate response. Your attacker is most likely to be within conversational distance (perhaps much closer), and the point at which you recognize the attack is also the point where you need to have an operational firearm in your hand. Having an un-chambered pistol under those circumstances may cost you time you don't have.

The concealed handgun is also the firearm of choice in circumstances where you may have only one hand free to operate the gun. The other hand may be busy doing something else relevant to your defense — including being injured — which precludes manually chambering a round.

With the close proximity of the threat comes the danger of your attacker stopping even a well-rehearsed chambering sequence. The chance of having the un-chambered handgun taken from you before you can put it into operating condition is higher than if the gun comes out of the holster ready to be fired by one hand.

Perimeter defense is very different. You already know there's a situation where lethal force is necessary. That's why you're running to retrieve the rifle. You also know quite a bit about the incident: You know who or what the attacker looks like, what it's doing, who's in danger, approximately where everyone is, and you have probably already worked out the basics of a plan to stop the attack.

The immediate shock of the first few seconds of a defensive incident is likely to be gone, and along with it a lot of the physiological responses to danger that affect how you train with a defensive handgun. You've had time to drop anything that might have been in your hands, and you have some space between you and the attacker to get the rifle into a shooting position.

The unique circumstances of perimeter defense give you the time to get your rifle into an operational state. It's unlike the "in your face" attacks that characterize the use of the legally carried defensive handgun. They are different tools used under different circumstances, even if their purpose (to protect innocent life) is the same.

With the rifle, chamber a round when you get to the point where you're likely to need to shoot.

*A word about ear protection*

A rifle generates a very loud sound, capable of causing ear damage (especially in close quarters). Whenever you shoot your rifle, you should wear proper hearing protection. Hearing damage is cumulative and irreversible, so it makes sense to take such precautions.

What about during a defensive incident? The danger of hearing damage doesn't go away just because it's an emergency. You'll still be damaging your ears every time you shoot. It makes sense to put on hearing protection as part of your retrieval process, and to this end, I stage a set of earmuffs with my rifle.

That being said, I also know I'm unlikely to grab them in an emergency. Going back to the fire extinguisher story, the chances are very good that I'm not going to take the time to put the earmuffs on. But I still stage them with my rifle and practice putting them on as part of the retrieval process, and I recommend you do the same.

---

\* - *If in doubt, re-read the first chapter on safety.*


\*\* - *Every bolt-action rifle I've handled operates in this manner. If in doubt, consult your owner's manual.*


\*\*\* - *If your rifle is also expected to serve as a defensive tool inside your home, the point of employment in that scenario may in fact be the same as the point of retrieval. Your assessment of the situation determines where the point of employment is, not some dogmatic measurement.*

*Chapter Eleven*
## HANDLING THE RIFLE

Each rifle design, from bolt-action to lever-action to semiautomatic, has its own particular method of handling and operation, or "manual of arms."* I will not try to recreate your rifle's instruction manual here, but rather give you some general guidelines for handling and operation in a defensive context.

I strongly encourage you to study your rifle's instruction manual to learn its specific handling and maintenance requirements. If you don't have the instruction manual, virtually all manufacturers will be happy to supply one for you. Many manufacturers have manuals online, and you can find internet resources for manuals from long-discontinued firearms.**

### Semiautomatic rifles

Semiautomatic rifles are the most popular type of rifle sold today, largely due to the tremendous sales success of AR-15-pattern guns. Their modularity, ease of modification and accessorization, and increasingly affordable prices have made them the single best-selling rifle in this country for the last decade. As a result, more people choose the AR-15 (and its larger brother, the AR-10) as a perimeter defense tool than probably all others.

Whether you have an AR pattern or some other semiautomatic rifle, the principles of handling are basically the same. In this discussion, I'll be assuming that your rifle has a detachable box magazine, which virtually all semiautomatic centerfire rifles do. Those that don't usually have either tubular magazines, whose handling is similar to lever-action rifles, or a box magazine with a hinged floorplate, which are covered in the section about bolt-action rifles.

All semiautomatic rifles have some sort of safety that is conveniently located for efficient operation. The only common exception I can think of is the Soviet AK-pattern rifle, whose safety is the least ergonomic and convenient of any rifle I've used. \*\*\*

The safety should always be on, except when you're actually shooting. Part of your practice should be focused on developing the skill of applying the safety, or checking that it's applied, whenever you pick the rifle up, load it, or have finished a string of fire.

The safety should also be on when the rifle is in storage/staging. Rifles should be stored with an empty chamber and the hammer down on the empty chamber, but some rifles (most notably the AR-15 pattern) don't allow you to apply the safety when the hammer is down. For those rifles, pay particular attention to applying the safety instantly after cycling the bolt to load. For others, develop the habit of checking that the safety is on any time you're handling or manipulating the rifle.

*Loading the semiautomatic rifle to cruiser ready*

The state of cruiser ready is characterized by a full magazine with an empty chamber and the safety on (where possible). As noted in the section on storage and retrieval, this is the preferred state for a defensive rifle.

To put a semiautomatic into cruiser ready, remove the magazine (if there's one in the rifle). Pull back the bolt and lock it into position by whatever means the rifle provides. Check that no magazine is in the gun and the chamber is empty. Then double-check it all again.

Point the muzzle in a safe direction and let the bolt down on the empty chamber. (Being the cautious sort, at this point I pull the bolt partway back and look into the chamber just to make sure it's empty. As my teaching colleague Georges Rahbani is fond of saying, "Seemingly obsessive concern with safety is the mark of the professional gun-handler.").

Once you're sure the chamber is empty, let the bolt all the way forward again. Keeping the gun pointed in a safe direction, take off the safety and pull the trigger to dry fire the rifle on the empty chamber. Doing so verifies that the chamber is empty and the hammer is in the decocked position, which is how it should be stored. If possible, put the safety back in the "on" position.

Now you can insert the loaded magazine into the rifle. You may find it quite difficult to latch in place, as the rounds need to be depressed slightly in the magazine as the top round contacts the bottom of the closed bolt. Usually this can be overcome by giving the magazine a sharp rap with the heel of your palm, driving it home. Some higher-capacity magazines, like the 30-round style for the AR-15, can't be seated easily, even when hitting it quite hard. In those cases, it's advisable to remove a round or two from the magazine to make seating easier.

Once the magazine is seated, give it a firm tug to make sure it is indeed latched into the rifle. Many times my students have been convinced that their magazine had been seated properly, only to have it fall out of the rifle when they fired the first shot! This extra tugging maneuver adds another layer of confidence that your rifle is in fact loaded and ready for action.

*Emergency reload*

The magazine capacity of most semiautomatic rifles makes emergency reloading a low-probability event. It's almost impossible to find a case of private-sector self-defense using a handgun where a reload was needed, and virtually none where it affected the outcome of the incident****. In spite of this reality, the emergency reload continues to be a major part of most rifle curricula these days, and some words on accomplishing it relatively efficiently are in order.

The emergency reload assumes that you've shot the magazine empty and are now faced with the desperate need for more ammunition. When you recognize the need to reload, drop the empty magazine from the gun and retrieve a new magazine. Insert the new magazine into the rifle and release the bolt to chamber a new round. That's it.

Partisans in the shooting community argue endlessly about exactly how you do this. Do you release the empty magazine first or when you have the spare magazine in your hand? Which hand does which task? Do you use the bolt catch to chamber a round, or do you use the bolt handle to manually cycle the action?

All of those are dependent on the rifle in question. For instance, if your perimeter defense rifle is of the AK (Soviet) pattern (or just about any variant), there is no bolt release, because the bolt doesn't lock open on an empty magazine. In that case, your only choice is to use the charging handle to cycle the bolt.

If you have a Steyr AUG bullpup, it's effectively impossible to release the empty magazine with one hand while the other is retrieving the spare magazine. The method usually taught is to retrieve the spare magazine with the support hand, use it to hit the large magazine release and drop the empty magazine, then insert the magazine into the rifle. Some models of this rifle have no bolt release, and so the conveniently placed charging handle is used to chamber a new round.

If you've already learned an emergency reload technique, I won't ask you to modify it in any way. The plausibility of need isn't high enough to justify the time it would take you to retrain. For everyone else, the procedure boils down to:

- Get the empty magazine out of the gun
- Insert the full magazine

- Chamber a round

To a large extent, your rifle dictates how you do those things. Do each step as efficiently as possible; if in doubt, you can find lots of different ways (along with lots of arguments as to which is best) on the internet. Just pick one: The reality is that it really doesn't matter, because it's a skill you're unlikely to need even on your worst day.

The only requirement I'll impose on you is to keep the muzzle pointed in a safe direction as you reload the rifle. Many people point the muzzle in the air when loading their gun, which is a patently unsafe method. More than once, I've observed rounds being ignited as they were chambered. Luckily in almost all cases, the rifle was pointed safely at a berm on a range, but accidents and deaths have been reported from incidents where the muzzle direction was not properly controlled.

Always keep the muzzle pointed in a generally safe direction when you're reloading (or even loading) your rifle. The rest of the procedure is of far less importance.

*Unloading*

Semiautomatic rifles with detachable box magazines are simple to unload. First, make sure the safety is engaged and the muzzle is pointed in a safe direction, then remove the magazine from the rifle and set it aside. Operate the bolt handle to eject any round still in the chamber. Pull the bolt back three times, just to be sure, then lock it open.

Inspect the chamber and magazine well to ensure there is no ammunition in the rifle, then close the bolt. If the rifle is to be stored for any length of time, keep the muzzle pointed in a safe direction and dry fire the rifle (pull the trigger to drop the hammer on an empty chamber). Apply the safety when you're finished (if your rifle's design allows it).

*Shooting the semiautomatic rifle*

As you reach the point of employment, if you're carrying the rifle with the muzzle up, lower the muzzle so it is pointed in a safe direction and quickly operate the bolt handle to chamber a round. Unless you're going to shoot immediately, put the safety on.

A point about chambering the semiautomatic rifle: When you operate the bolt handle, release it completely from your hand. Many people ride the bolt handle forward as the round chambers, and with some rifle designs, this can result in the round not fully chambering — or even an actual jam that must be cleared. Only by letting the bolt go forward completely under its own power can this be avoided.

Operate the bolt as you would a bow and arrow: Release the handle and allow it to fly forward completely on its own. In classes, I teach my students that their hand should actually move backward a little after they've released the bolt. This ensures the bolt was brought back as far as its design would allow and definitely released completely.

When you've made the decision to shoot and are shouldering the rifle is the time to take the safety off. If your rifle has its safety inside the trigger guard, you'll have to make a conscious effort to keep your finger away from the trigger until the rifle butt has made contact with your shoulder. I've seen many premature discharges before the rifle was properly shouldered, and they almost always result in a miss. Control your trigger finger!

After you've fired and have decided that no more shots are necessary, put the safety on. Practice consciously to make a solid habit of reflexively putting on the safety immediately after you've stopped shooting.

For semiautomatic rifles with pistol grips, your shooting hand should be as high up on the grip as possible. This usually puts your hand in the perfect position to manipulate the trigger, because it's where your trigger finger can apply straight pressure to the trigger. This allows the trigger to move back without any sideways pressure, which keeps the trigger finger from steering the muzzle and greatly aids precise shooting.

Some rifles inexplicably come with grips that prevent doing so; the standard A2 grip of the AR-15, with its "shelf" between the fingers, is one such example. Fortunately, aftermarket grips for AR-pattern rifles will allow you to better position your shooting hand. If you have hands that deviate in either direction from "average," I highly recommend these aftermarket grips.

**Lever-action rifles**

The lever-action rifle was once the most popular hunting arm in the country, in no small part due to its simple manual of arms. It's easy to operate, reliable, and robust — just what people on the frontier needed in a multipurpose tool. Those qualities haven't changed, making the lever-action a viable choice for a defensive tool today.

*Loading the lever-action to cruiser ready*

First, make sure the rifle is unloaded. Operate the lever to open the action, and leave it open; check to be sure a round is not in the chamber. Close the action, then immediately open it again and double-check everything. Make sure the gun is truly empty.

Once you've done that, close the action. You now need to decock the rifle. If it has an external hammer, as most lever-actions do, point the gun in a safe direction and hold the hammer back with your thumb. At the same time, pull the trigger to release the hammer. Controlling the hammer with your thumb, allow it to ride slowly into its rest (fired) position. If your rifle has a safety, move it to the safe position.

If your gun is one of the rare examples that has a hidden or enclosed hammer, after you've verified and double-checked that the chamber and magazine are empty, close the action with the lever. Point the muzzle in a safe direction and dry fire the gun by pulling the trigger. The hammer will drop into its rest position. Do not operate the lever again! Leave the rifle in the "fired" state so you can load the magazine and apply the safety.

Once you've verified the chamber is empty and the rifle has been decocked, you're ready to load the magazine.

While a few lever-action rifles have been made with conventional box magazines, they're in the extreme minority compared to the under-barrel tubular magazines that almost define the design. Most tubular magazines, at least for centerfire cartridges, load from a small port — called a gate — on the side of the rifle's receiver.

Loading through the gate is simplicity itself: Take one round and push it against the gate's cover. The cover will depress inward and let you push the round into the magazine. Push another round into the gate behind it and repeat until you've filled the magazine and the gate snaps closed. The rifle is ready to fire.

A very few lever-actions, mostly those shooting rimfire cartridges like the .22 Long Rifle, load through a port in the magazine tube itself. In order to load, you must unlatch and pull the magazine insert (called a follower) out of the tube until the port is open. This requires you to put your hand in front of the muzzle, which is a dangerous maneuver.

Because of that safety issue, I recommend you never reload a tube-port rifle unless it is completely empty. Make sure the chamber is clear and the hammer is not cocked. Once you've verified that you have an empty rifle, unlatch the follower and pull it out until the port opens. Then simply drop rounds into the magazine tube until it's full, push the follower back into the tube, and latch it in place.

When loading through the magazine port, pay particular attention that the rounds are going into the tube in the proper orientation. The cartridge base goes in first, with the bullet pointing toward the muzzle. Getting one in backward will likely jam the rifle.

You should now have a rifle with a full magazine, an empty chamber, and the hammer down on that empty chamber. It's ready for storage or staging.

*(Special procedure for early Savage 99 models:* While later Savage 99s came with a detachable box magazine, the early guns had an integral rotary magazine that can only be loaded with the action open. This makes it

difficult and a little dangerous to load to cruiser ready. If you're stuck with one as your defensive rifle, the loading procedure is a bit different. Open the action and insert rounds into the magazine, pushing each in until it is caught by the rotor.

When it has been completely filled, use your thumb to hold the top round down so you can close the action. This requires a bit of coordination to keep your thumb from being pinched in the action. Once the action is closed, apply the safety. The rifle now has a full magazine and an empty chamber.

Unless you are on a range with a proper backstop and ear protection, do not attempt to drop the hammer on the empty chamber. Leave it in the cocked position with the safety on.)

*Emergency reload*

It's unlikely that you'd need to reload the rifle because it ran out of ammunition, but should that occur, the lever-action is easy to load "on the fly." Simply swing the lever down so the action is open, drop a single round into the gun, close the lever, and fire. This works with the predominant designs from Winchester and Marlin, rifles based on those classic designs, and even oddities like the long-discontinued Savage Model 99.

Critics will point out it's only a single round, but at the same time, loading the gun any other way is slow. The reality is that, for virtually all plausible perimeter defense scenarios, the ammunition in the magazine is going to be enough. In the event that the universe somehow conspires against you and it isn't, the emergency reload should see you through.

*Unloading*

If there is one area where the lever-action is clearly inferior to other designs, it's in unloading. With the common tubular magazine, it's a fiddly process that takes a surprisingly long time to accomplish.

To unload the typical lever-action, it's useful to turn the gun upside down, so the top of the rifle is facing the ground. Keep the muzzle pointed in a safe direction and operate the lever without touching the trigger. (Having the gun upside down makes it nearly impossible for your trained forefinger to get to and reflexively pull the trigger.)

Operate the lever briskly and eject every round onto the ground until there are no more. When you believe the rifle to be empty, turn it right-side up and check the chamber. Operate the lever again to double-check you didn't miss an errant round. When you're satisfied the gun is empty, close the action and, keeping the muzzle pointed in a safe direction, decock the hammer.

The exceptions to this procedure are those rare lever-actions that have detachable magazines. The unloading process is much easier: Take out the magazine, operate the lever to eject any round in the chamber, then double-check that the chamber is empty by operating the action twice more before closing the action and safely decocking the hammer.

If you are sufficiently coordinated, you can hold your hand under the action as the rounds are ejected and catch them. This makes it a little difficult to operate the action while still stabilizing the rifle, and I recommend it only if you've practiced the procedure in a safe area (such as on a range).

*Shooting the lever-action*

In the heyday of the lever-action, rifles didn't have safeties in the sense that we know them today. The only safety for a lever-action was to lower the hammer to half-cock, a procedure that was risky under the best of circumstances. While most lever-actions being produced today usually have some sort of built-in safety, those made just a few decades ago still held to the traditional safety-less patterns.

Safeties on modern lever-actions have usually been retrofitted to the existing rifle designs and really aren't optimized for easy access while in a shooting position*****. As a result, the manual of arms for the lever-action has almost always included chambering a round just before shooting, as part of the shouldering process.

As you confirm your target and make the decision to shoot, begin to level your rifle and bring it to your shoulder. As the rifle comes to a position roughly parallel to the ground, operate the lever to chamber a round. As the action closes, bring your thumb into position on the top of the stock, just to one side of the centerline and pointed parallel to the barrel. The thumb should not cross the centerline of the stock, but stay alongside the hammer or tang.

Continue to bring the rifle solidly into your shoulder pocket, move your trigger finger onto the trigger, and fire the shot. If you need to fire another round, open your shooting hand wide, push forward to operate the lever, then bring the lever back and close your hand on the gun — remembering your proper thumb position.

Having the thumb alongside the stock, rather than wrapped over or around it, makes operating the lever much faster and less likely to jar the gun off target.

It used to be (and in some circles still is) doctrinal to *always* operate the lever and chamber a new round immediately after firing, while the gun is still recovering from recoil. The idea is to be ready to fire another round immediately, in the same way the semiautomatic rifle is always ready to shoot. This notion is reinforced in some schools by shooting tests that are designed around the rapid fire of the self-loading rifle and penalize manually cycled rifles for having a comparatively slow rate of fire.

Back in the world where you and I live, I just don't believe it to be absolutely necessary for most plausible defensive scenarios. Your shots shouldn't be directed by a reflex born of unrealistic training and fantasy, but rather a deliberate decision whose efficient execution is made possible by practiced skills.

Even in cases where multiple attackers, such as fast-moving packs of feral dogs, are involved, there is sufficient time to evaluate the situation and decide to (or not to) make another shot. That decision may in fact be made before the first shot is fired, but always held in check by your continuous assessment of the scene. If that second (or third) shot is still necessary, then you can operate the action to chamber and fire another round.

**Bolt-action rifles**

The bolt-action rifle in many ways parallels the operation of the lever-action rifle. They're both manually operated repeaters, usually without detachable magazines, that have a slow rate of fire compared to semi-automatic firearms —for which they are routinely denigrated and penalized in military-fantasy rifle training classes.

Yet the bolt-action remains the rifle design with the best potential for high precision. It's robust, has the fewest moving parts of any repeating rifle design, and is well understood by generations of hunters and target shooters.

Though there are rare exceptions, most bolt-actions come with one of three types of magazines: the detachable box, much like that of a semi-automatic rifle; an internal magazine with a hinged floorplate for easy unloading; or an internal magazine without a floorplate, usually called a "blind" magazine.

*Loading the bolt-action to cruiser ready*

First it's necessary to understand how the bolt-action is properly decocked. Because bolt-actions use a striker contained in the bolt, rather than an external hammer, it's not easily thumbed down like a lever-action. Instead, the striker has to be released as the bolt is rotated to its locked position. It's a little awkward to do, but once learned and practiced, it becomes much easier.

Ensure the chamber is empty and the muzzle is pointed in a safe direction. Push the bolt fully forward but do not turn the handle down. Depress the trigger and hold it in the fully back position, then rotate the bolt down and release the trigger. This will lower the striker slowly so it is not damaged. (This method works for all commercial bolt-actions with which I'm familiar, both rimfire and centerfire, but there may be some antique or obscure military arms for which it doesn't.)

Once you understand how to properly decock the striker and have practiced the procedure with a completely empty rifle, you can safely put it into a cruiser-ready state.

For those rifles with detachable magazines, after closing the bolt on a verified empty chamber, simply insert the filled magazine. Make sure it's completely seated and latched in. The force of the top round being pushed against the bolt by the magazine spring can sometimes make this difficult without applying some force.

If your magazine has a hinged floorplate, after verifying the empty chamber, just open the bottom, drop in the correct number of rounds (making sure their projectiles point forward), and close the plate. Again, make sure it's properly latched in place.

The blind magazine will only load through the open action, which means the bolt has to be pulled back. Push the correct number of rounds into the magazine, then while pushing the ammunition down with your thumb, push the bolt forward so that no round is picked up and pushed into the chamber. After pushing the bolt forward, follow the procedure for decocking on an empty chamber.

Bolt-actions with blind magazines require strict adherence to procedure and conscious checking to make sure you don't accidentally chamber a round you didn't intend to chamber. They're also awkward, particularly if you have a scope mounted over the action.

I prefer bolt-action rifles where the bolt can be cycled with the safety on, and recommend that rifles so equipped be stored chamber empty with the safety on. This gives an added layer of security when handling and cycling in a stressful situation. If your bolt-action safety also locks the bolt, preventing its cycling, then I recommend storing it with the safety off.

In all cases, of course, the rifle should be stored with the striker forward — its spring relaxed — as described previously.

*The emergency reload*

Like the lever-action, should you run out of ammunition, the fastest way to reload is just to open the bolt and drop a fresh round into the open action. With many (though not all) bolt-action rifles, there's no need to push it into the magazine; simply drop it into the action and close the bolt. If your rifle is of the type which locks the bolt in the open position when the magazine is empty, you'll need to push the round into the magazine to allow the bolt to close and chamber the round.

Again, this procedure is a little more difficult if you have a scope mounted over the action (as most bolt-action rifles are designed). If there's no scope in the way, the round can almost be thrown into the action without regard for the exact angle or direction. But with a scope, you need to be careful to tip the rifle slightly so the opening between the scope and action is pointed slightly upward, at which point you can drop in the round, rotate the rifle so it's upright, then close the bolt to chamber the round.

*Unloading*

For rifles with detachable magazines, remove the magazine and open the bolt to eject any chambered round. Do this twice to verify that the gun is empty.

Rifles with hinged floorplates are almost as easy: Open the floorplate and let the rounds in the magazine fall out. Close the floorplate and open the bolt to eject any chambered round, then double-check the chamber and the magazine to ensure there is no stray ammunition.

In both cases, close the bolt and decock the striker. (The striker should always be decocked for storage.)

Rifles with blind magazines are a little more difficult because, like the lever-action, the rounds must be cycled through the action to remove them. To do this, open the bolt to eject any chambered round, then push the bolt forward again — but do not turn the bolt to lock. The bolt will pick up a round from the magazine and then push it into the chamber; if you stop short of fully chambered, you can just pull the bolt back, which will eject the live round. Repeat this push-pull action until the magazine is empty, then verify the empty magazine and chamber before decocking the gun.

It's necessary to keep the muzzle pointed in a safe direction for the entire procedure. If your rifle allows the bolt to open with the safety on (not all do), it's best to apply the safety before unloading. This gives another layer of redundancy should you lock the bolt down with a live round in the chamber.

*Shooting the bolt-action*

Like the lever-action, the bolt-action is manually operated between shots, but the bolt-action operation is a bit slower and more complex than the lever-action.

Another difference between the two is that the bolt-action rifle has, with few exceptions, always incorporated a safety of some sort. In virtually all cases, the safety is on the centerline of the gun, either on the bolt itself or on the tang (the piece of metal behind the bolt to which the buttstock is attached).

As a result, the bolt-action benefits even more from keeping the shooting-hand thumb on the centerline — or just to one side — of the rifle. Rather than wrapping the thumb around the stock, as most people seem to do, the shooting-hand thumb should be pointed toward the target and simply laid on the tang or on the stock to the side of the tang.

This gives you easy access to the safety, no matter where it's located, and makes the manipulation of the bolt a bit smoother and faster.

When you've retrieved the rifle and arrived at the spot where you'll likely need to shoot, cycle the action to load a round into the chamber.

If your rifle is of the type where the safety locks the bolt, and the situation is such that you're not going to immediately shoot, I recommend that you flip the safety on.

Should you need to shoot, as you start to shoulder the rifle, get in the habit of flipping the safety off. For those rifles whose safety is on the bolt, this can happen as soon as the rifle is parallel to the ground and roughly pointed at the target. For those rifles where the safety is on the tang, take it off just before your finger enters the trigger guard.

Should you need to fire a second shot, take your finger out of the trigger guard, open your hand so your other fingers aren't grasping the stock, and rotate your hand so the bolt comes into the space between your thumb and forefinger. Depending on the exact configuration of your rifle and your own physiology, you may be able to merely rotate your wrist up and back with the bolt riding in the slot formed by those fingers — the bolt acting something like a cam in a raceway. Rotate it back all the way to eject the empty casing, then reverse the movement to push the bolt forward and down to lock. Re-establish your shooting grasp.

Unfortunately, I have short arms and small hands, and have personally never owned a centerfire rifle where I could do that! Instead I've always ended up grasping the bolt knob between my thumb and forefinger, forming a little pocket where the bolt rides as I pull it back and push it forward again.

The key to operating the bolt smoothly and rapidly is to not involve your elbow. If you'll forgive the cliché, "It's all in the wrist." If your elbow comes up as you operate the bolt, pay closer attention to how you're trapping or grasping the bolt; it should be allowed to rotate in your hand, the hand simply guiding it as it moves up and down, back and forth.

Left handed shooters will need to develop the technique of reaching over the rifle with their shooting hand to operate the bolt. I've seen many 'lefties' who can do so quite rapidly.

Again, as with the lever-action, the decision to chamber another round should be a deliberate action prompted by your recognition of the need to shoot again.

## Handling the rifle when the police arrive

Unless a suspect has committed a heinous crime, such as murder, I don't recommend trying to hold anyone at gunpoint for the police. If a petty thief wants to run away at the sight of your rifle, let him run. Holding him at gunpoint raises many legal and practical issues, and it's best to avoid those whenever possible.

It's not possible to predict every incident, however, and circumstances may result in you holding your rifle on a suspect when the police arrive. It's best if you safely disarm prior to the officers exiting their vehicles, guns in hand and pointed at you. Holding a firearm when they arrive puts you in the position of looking very much like a bad guy on a call where they may have been told nothing more than "shots fired."

Many in the defensive training world are convinced this is the reason to have a sling on the rifle. They say you can simply hang the rifle on your shoulder when the police get on scene, keeping it under your control while at the same time reducing the appearance of risk.

I'm not sure it's always the case. The police officers I've queried have told me they don't necessarily regard the slung rifle as always being an indicator of safety for them, and depending on the totality of the circumstances, they may be likely to order the person to put the rifle on the ground and step away from it.

If that's the likely course of action, perhaps it's best to plan ahead to do so quickly and safely — before needing to be told at gunpoint. The question is how to do it and maintain both your safety and that of the responding officers.

*Keep it away from the bad guy*

It's imperative that the person you're covering can't get to your rifle and use it against you or the officers, so it's a good idea to back off from the suspect before the police get there. Since perimeter defense by definition occurs at distances greater than arm's reach, this shouldn't be an issue, but I realize humanity (or the nature of the incident itself) sometimes results in being relatively close to a suspect.

If that's the case, once you've established control or ascertained the suspect's condition and called for help, it's a good idea to back off to a safe distance — where you can both observe and maintain control over the scene without the risk of the suspect charging you and gaining control of your rifle. If obstacles such as fences or vehicles are between you, they will greatly reduce the chances of him being able to physically assault you and take your gun.

If the suspect was armed, pay particular attention to putting something between you that will reduce the chances of him being able to shoot you. Look for something in your environment that will stop (or greatly alter the flight of) a bullet. A car may not always do that job, but hiding on the other side of the car's engine is likely to. A tractor or other farm equipment is generally much heavier in construction than an automobile and will stop almost anything fired at it. Large trees usually serve the same purpose.

If you position yourself with care, when the police arrive and force you to disarm, you won't be in immediate danger from a newly emboldened suspect.

### *Unload the rifle*

As the police arrive, you need to do two things — quickly unload the rifle and step away from it so the police can see you're not a threat to them.

If you're using a semiautomatic rifle with a detachable magazine, push the magazine release and let the magazine fall to the ground. Don't pick it up; just leave it. Once you've done that, operate the bolt to eject any round that happens to be in the chamber. Again, let it fall to the ground. Lock the bolt back only if you can do it very quickly and without fumbling. The longer the gun is in your hands, the more likely it is that the officers will feel threatened.

If you're using a bolt-action with a fixed magazine, push the floorplate catch and let the rounds in the magazine fall clear. Quickly open the bolt, ejecting the round in the chamber, and leave it open.

Lever-actions or bolt-actions with blind magazines (those without a floorplate) are handled in the same manner. Open the action, ejecting the round in the chamber, and leave the action open. Ammunition will still be in the magazine, but the important point is that the action is open, conveying the message that it doesn't present an immediate danger to the officers.

*Ground the rifle*

Now it's time to get the gun out of your hands. Naturally you want to treat the rifle carefully, while at the same time the responding officers aren't likely to care if your prized gun gets scratched up or even broken in the process.

Quickly lay the rifle down and back away from it. You might put it on the ground or perhaps on a car hood or the top of a stone wall or farm implement. Don't walk around looking for a place to put the gun, or move somewhere that's "better" for the condition of your rifle. Wherever you are, get the gun out of your hands immediately.

Pay some attention to the direction of the muzzle when you lay the rifle down. Ideally, you don't want it pointed at the responding officers. That might mean pointing it in a direction you normally wouldn't. From the officers' perspective, anywhere other than at them is a safe direction.

Again, once the rifle is out of your hands, back away from it. The first thing you need to demonstrate to the officers is that you're not a threat to them. Discussing who the actual bad guy is and what he's done to warrant your use of your rifle needs to wait until after they've secured the scene and you've talked with your attorney. In the meantime, don't pose a threat to their immediate safety and follow their instructions without hesitation. Sort out the details after everyone has calmed down.

---

\* - *This term comes to us from the 18$^{th}$ century, when it referred to the instruction book for handling and using weapons in the field. Because early matchlock and flintlock rifles had a complex loading and firing sequence, it was necessary to codify the procedure in a manual of arms, which would then serve as the training manual.*

\*\* - *Two large repositories of firearm instruction manuals on the 'net:*

www.stevespages.com/page7b.htm

pdf.textfiles.com/manuals/FIREARMS/

\*\*\* - *While fans of the AK-style safety defend it vociferously, the fact remains it's an ergonomically poor design, no matter how much invective is hurled at the person with the temerity to point out that fact.*

\*\*\*\* - *Most cases used as proof of the vital need for reloading skills involve people who had knowingly been marked for attack by organized criminals. If you've incited the ire of such a group, I'll concede that you probably need to practice emergency reloads. For everyone else, it's hard to justify the time and effort.*

\*\*\*\*\* - *Only the current production Winchester lever-action rifles, with their tang safeties, are usable in a shooting position, the way modern shooters have learned to use safeties.*

*Chapter Twelve*

# ZEROING THE RIFLE

If there is anything like a mystery about the rifle, it's the zero. One of the most common rifle questions I get is, "What zero do you use?" Everyone has their favorite zero, and endless internet debates abound regarding what zero is "best." You can find references to the "Army zero," and "Marine zero," and arguments about which one is better.

Underlying all that static is a persistent belief that if they only get the right zero, they'll instantly and magically become better shooters.

It's all quite silly, because the zero isn't nearly as important as people make it out to be. In principle, it's very simple, and you learned everything you need to know about it when you were a child.

## What is a "zero"?

When you were a kid, you probably played with the garden hose, and perhaps you even used it to soak a brother, sister, or unlucky playmate. You no doubt learned very quickly that if you held the garden hose parallel to the ground, the stream would arc toward the earth instead of your intended victim. Even if you stuck your thumb over the end of the hose, increasing the pressure of the stream, gravity started pulling on the water molecules as soon as they exited the nozzle, and the water stream was quickly brought to earth.

How did you solve the problem? You raised the nozzle so the arc of the water intersected with your line of sight to your target, and when you reached just the right angle, you heard a satisfying scream from the suddenly wet victim.

The rifle works exactly the same way.

If the barrel of the rifle is held parallel to flat ground, when a round is fired, the bullet comes out of the barrel and is instantly affected by the gravitational pull of the earth. The acceleration of gravity, that is the rate at which the bullet is pulled to earth, is a function of time — not of distance. The longer the bullet is in the air, the more it is affected by gravity. During the time of the bullet's flight, it gets farther from its starting point, so the farther the bullet travels, the more its path is affected by gravity. At some point, it will hit the ground, because gravity has pulled it there.

The problem is that our vision isn't affected by gravitational forces. We see in a straight line, and as we look at the target, the line of our vision doesn't curve like the bullet's path does. The result is that our parallel-to-the-ground rifle doesn't match our line of sight, and the bullet can't hit the target unless it's immediately in front of the muzzle.

When you adjust your sights to zero the rifle, you're actually adjusting the angle of the barrel relative to your line of sight. The goal is to get the barrel angled just enough to launch the bullet on an arc (trajectory) that causes it to meet your line of sight. At that point, your line of sight and the bullet's impact coincide. The exact amount of the angle determines how far from the muzzle that point is:

# PROTECTING YOUR HOMESTEAD

A rifle zero, then, is simply the distance at which the bullet intersects with your line of sight — where it will hit exactly where you aim. That's all there is to it. You're matching the arc of the bullet to your line of sight by adjusting the angle at which the barrel sits, just as you intuitively matched the stream of water to hit your brother/sister/former friend.

Depending on the distance chosen, you'll either have a single zero at the top of the bullet's arc ...

... or two zeros, the first as the bullet's trajectory takes it through your line of sight, the second as it comes down:

It's really not that complicated. If ever in doubt, think back to your adventures with the garden hose. The principles are the same, even though the actual parameters differ greatly.

*Height over bore*

The design of your rifle is going to greatly affect the arc necessary to make the bullet hit where you're looking. Thinking back to the garden hose, if you held the nozzle at hip height, you had to angle it more — give the water stream a high arc — to match your view of your target than if you held the nozzle closer to your head.

Rifles are the same. Rifles have what's known as "height over bore" (HOB) — the distance between the top of the sights (or the red dot or the scope crosshairs) and the center of the barrel bore. Also called "sight height," the greater the HOB, the more it affects the trajectory necessary to hit where you're aiming within a likely defensive range.

Take, for instance, this bullet plot:

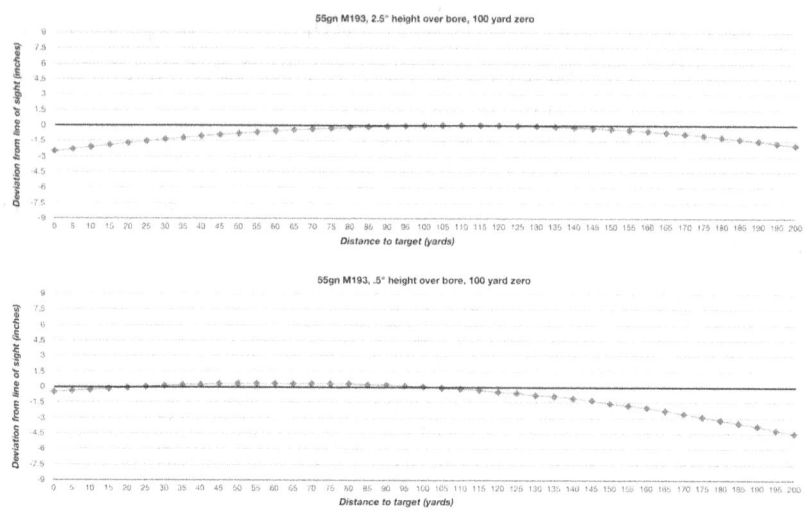

This is a ballistic plot of a .223/5.56 round, fired from a rifle with a low HOB (such as a bolt-action) and from one with a high HOB (such as an AR-15). Notice how the bullet's arc (the dotted line) changes to match the line of sight to the target, and how much steeper it is for the gun with the high HOB.

Now that you have a grasp of the concept, you can zero your rifle.

## What distance to zero your rifle?

The distance at which you zero will determine the angle of the barrel necessary to make the bullet land on target at that distance. As you've seen, the goal is to make the arc of the bullet intersect your line of sight at the desired distance: When the arc coincides with your aim point, you've achieved a zero at that distance.

If you're a target shooter trying to repeatedly hit a defined point at a defined distance, you'll adjust your zero to precisely match the distance at which you shoot. At any other distance, you apply adjustments to keep the bullet hitting in a very small area of precision. The choice of zero under those conditions is pretty cut and dried: Where's the target? Zero to match that distance.

As it happens, though, when you're using the rifle in self-defense (or even hunting), a considerable amount of leeway exists in where the bullet can land relative to where you're aiming and still be effective. If you're hunting deer, the area you need to hit is rather generous. Any bullet landing inside that area will have a very high expectation of causing the instant incapacitation necessary for a clean kill. Depending on the size of the deer, that area will be roughly eight to 10 inches in diameter. In hunting terms, that's called the "vital area."

If your sights are zeroed at 100 yards and the deer is at 150 yards, the chances are quite good (depending on the cartridge you're using) that the bullet's arc will still deliver the bullet into that vital area. At that distance, the deer is within what's known as "point-blank" range.

*What is point-blank range?*

Except in the aforementioned activity of competitive target shooting, you don't need the bullet to hit at exactly one precise point. What you need it to do is hit somewhere within the vital area of the target. That area is defined as one in which every bullet is roughly equal in effect to every other bullet. I refer to this as the area of precision, and it's dictated by the target.

If your target isn't a point but an area of precision, and every bullet into that area is equal to every other bullet, then you have little need to compensate for a small change in the bullet's trajectory by aiming high or low. As long as it lands in that area, you'll get the effect you want.

Back to our deer example: If your target has a vital area, an area of precision, that is eight inches in diameter, there is a range of distance

— a zone — in front of and behind your zero point where the bullet's arc will still carry it to a hit inside that vital area. Within that zone, you don't need to alter or worry about your aim point to compensate for trajectory. Aim in the center of that area, and the bullet will hit within it.

That zone is known as the point-blank range. When your target is within your point-blank range for the size of its vital area, you can simply place your sights in the center of that area and (assuming you hold the gun steady) the bullet will land inside of the vital area. The point-blank range is the distance at which you need no sight corrections to hit inside a target of a known size.

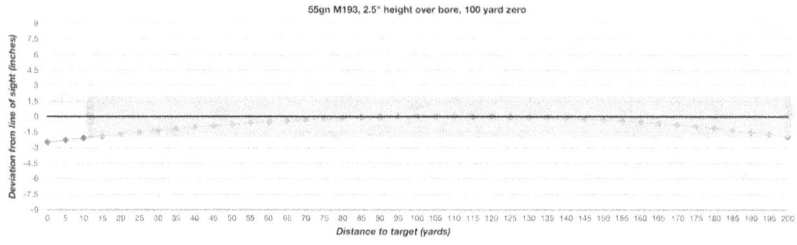

*The grey cylinder represents a target with a 4-inch diameter. If the aim point is in the center of that target area, if it's between about 12 yards and 200 yards from the rifle the bullet will hit inside of the area. This is the point-blank range for a target of that size.*

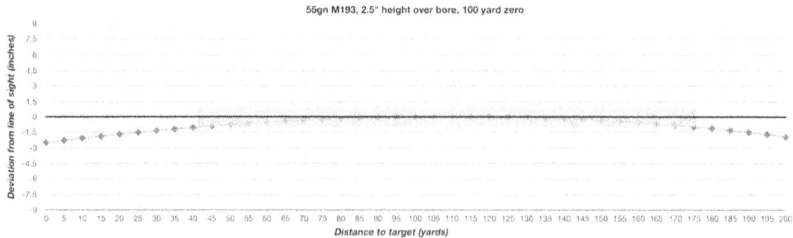

*The target size has been reduced to a 2-inch diameter; notice the point blank range has also decreased, from about 42 yards to 175 yards.*

For instance, if you're dealing with a feral dog attacking livestock, and the dog is standing broadside to you, the vital zone necessary to incapacitate the animal is probably around four inches (give or take) in diameter. If you hold in the center of that area, and the animal is inside of the point-blank range for your cartridge, you'll eliminate the threat without needing to think about adjusting where you're aiming. In the distances at which perimeter defense is likely to occur, understanding when you need to compensate for target range and when you don't is important.

As you can see, the point-blank range for any given target size is affected by the arc of the bullet. The shallower the arc, the greater your point-blank zone (the distance in front of and behind the point of aim) is. The more pronounced the arc, the smaller the point-blank range is. The larger the point-blank range, the less you need to worry about your bullet's trajectory — the task becomes "point and click."

For many rifle cartridges, the point-blank range is large enough that it will encompass the entire area across which you might expect to need your rifle.

*Point-blank and zero*

When people argue about zero ranges, what they're really arguing about is where and how big the point-blank zone is. Your choice of zero distance affects your point-blank range. When you're zeroing your rifle, you're picking the distance that gives you the point-blank zone you believe to be the best for your circumstances. Now that you understand this concept, the mystery of the "right" zero should be a mystery no more!

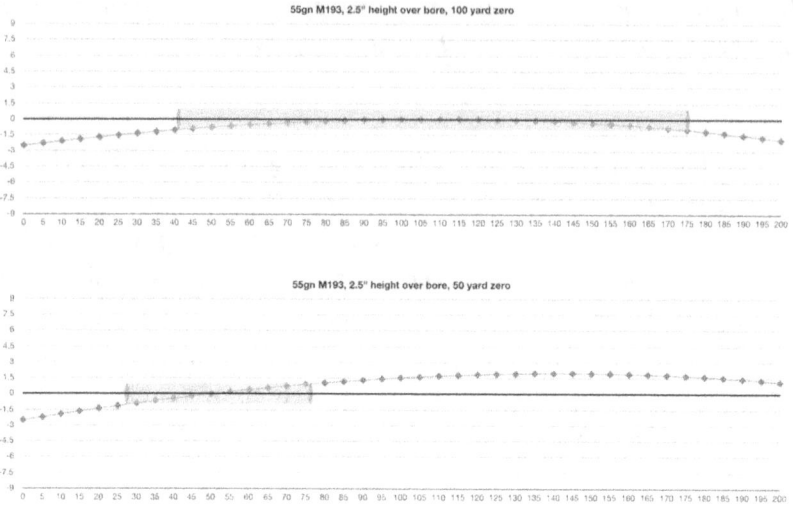

*Changing the zero range can dramatically affect the point-blank range for any given rifle/cartridge combination. Grey area represents a 2-inch target zone.*

Of course you need to decide what your point-blank range should be. Knowing the conditions under which you shoot, and what your expected threats will be, will make that decision easy. I'm going to suggest that you adjust your zero distance with the goal of maximizing the point-blank zone for common target sizes and expected distances.

For most of the threats you'll face in perimeter defense, I suggest that a vital area — an area of precision — of around four inches in diameter is a very workable assumption. A four-inch vital area will suffice for human and most animal predators. If you recognize that the area of precision of your target is smaller, you can then worry about compensating for the bullet trajectory.

### How height-over-bore affects the point-blank zone

Back to the height-over-bore (HOB) discussion: The greater the HOB of your rifle, the more it affects the gun's point-blank range. In general, the gun with the large HOB dimension will have a smaller point-blank zone than that of the rifle with the low HOB. Let's take another look at that plot of the .223/5.56 bullet fired from the two different rifles — a bolt-action and an AR-15 — and show the point-blank zones if they're both zeroed at 100 yards:

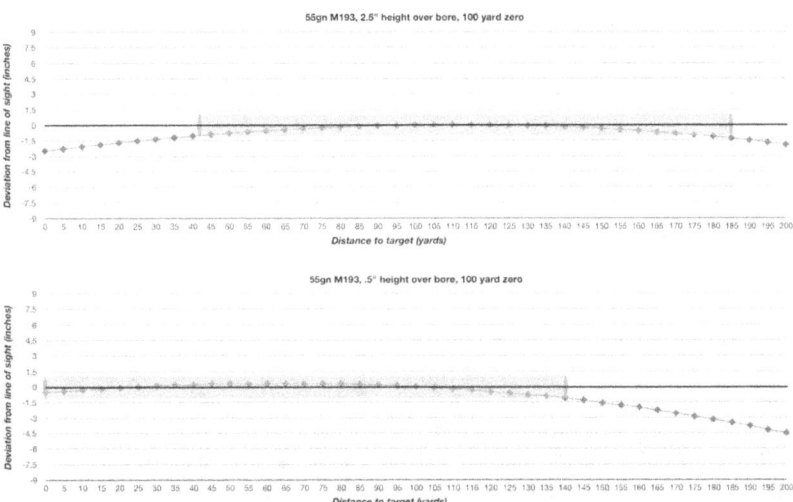

How about if we change the zero point from 100 yards to 50 yards?

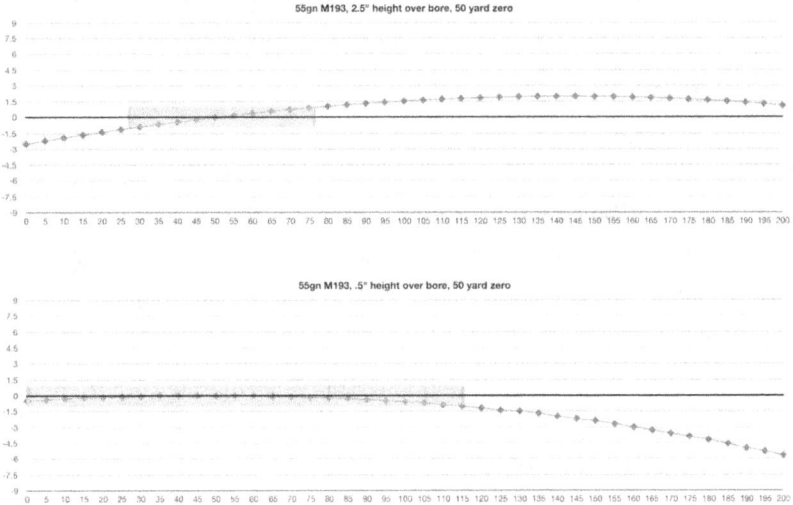

Notice how the point-blank zone changes?

The person shooting a bolt-action or lever-action rifle, with sights closer to the bore, will generally have a larger point-blank zone for any given cartridge, making it usable over a wider range. That's not the only factor in choosing a rifle/cartridge combination, but it's something to keep in mind!

### "Dual" zero

Much has been written about the dual zero and how magical it is. But if you understand a bullet's trajectory, it's really not so mysterious.

Most people choose to zero their rifle where the bullet arc just intersects their line of sight. The bullet arcs up to the line of sight, then arcs downward past the zero distance. If, however, you think in terms of maximizing your point-blank range, you can adjust your zero so the bullet arcs up and over your line of sight, then back down to pass through the line a second time.

Many refer to this as a "dual zero," because there are two points where the aim point will exactly match the bullet impact. Some will look at it as a way to zero their rifle for long distance (the second zero point) by using only a target at a specified short distance (the first zero point). But things don't always work out that way!

Zeroing at a close distance and expecting it to be exact at a farther distance requires careful plotting, using lots of ammunition and targets, of your bullet's trajectory out of your gun. Ballistic charts will get you close, sometimes remarkably so, but if you're expecting to win a shooting contest without shooting at the actual target distance, you're quite unlikely to succeed.

The only zero point about which you can be absolutely sure is the one where you see the bullets land on the target. The other should be considered an approximation. A pretty good one, but until you test it, you can't be absolutely sure. What the dual zero really gives you is a greater point-blank range, which is why it's useful.

**Sources of ballistic information**

My favorite online ballistics calculator comes from the Swedish ammunition manufacturer Norma. It's unique in that it shows you, interactively and graphically, how the trajectory changes with such things as zero range and height over bore. It is, by far, the best self-teaching tool I've found.

*www.norma.cc/en/Ammunition-Academy/Ballistics/ballistics-program/*

*Chapter Thirteen*

# ACCURACY, PRECISION, AND TIME

"Precision" and "accuracy" are two different terms (concepts, really) that are often confused for each other. Understanding the difference is important to developing your ability to hit a target when the pressure is on.

## Precision

Lots of people say "accuracy" when they really mean *precision*. Precision refers to the *area* of the target in which the shots need to be placed. When you're practicing or taking a training course, that area is the designated space on the target where every shot is worth exactly the same amount as every other shot. If your bullets hit within that area, and there is no smaller area delineated, you have been as precise as the target requires you to be.

Of course, in a defensive incident, your attacker doesn't give you the courtesy of having that area of precision spray-painted on his shirt! When applied to defensive shooting, precision refers to the area in which each shot will contribute the maximum amount to stopping the attack. You need to apply your skill (control over your rifle) to cause your rounds to land inside that area.

*Precision is recognized*

Whether you're shooting at paper targets, your next dinner, or a live threat, the target itself dictates the precision you need to deliver. It's your job to understand the level of precision the target dictates and then apply the level of skill necessary to put your bullets there. Precision, therefore, is *recognized*: You look at the target and determine what the area of precision is, and then recall how much skill you need to apply to hit inside that area of precision.

Of course, that determination process needs to happen very quickly. Your training and practice are what build that recognition-recall pattern, so you can look at a target at any given distance and know what you need to do to hit it.

## Accuracy

Accuracy, on the other hand, refers to whether or not any given shot actually hits within the area of precision you've recognized.

Accuracy is a digital concept. It is "yes" or "no" — you either hit within the area of precision or you didn't. If your shot hits within the area of precision, it is accurate. If it hits outside that area, it is not accurate. Either you delivered the precision needed, or you didn't.

Because accuracy means shooting to the required level of precision (as dictated by the target), there can be no such thing as "more accurate" or "less accurate." Shooting smaller groups means shooting to a greater degree of precision, but accuracy always refers to whether the precision was achieved.

Since you don't get to choose the area of precision, your job is to apply your skill to put the bullets into the area the target has dictated. The measurement of your success is whether you were able to.

**Time is short**

Can you choose to shoot to a greater level of precision than the target dictates? Certainly, and in fact a lot of training courses ask you to do just that, to shoot smaller and smaller groups inside of the target area. When you analyze it, though, that's not a particularly good way to approach the problem.

Think of it this way: If every bullet that hits into the area of precision is approximately equal in effect or value to every other one, spending more of your time and using more of your energy to shoot to an artificially higher level of precision gains you nothing for the expenditure. All you're doing is using more time (and energy) to get to the same end goal.

If you're shooting at the center of your attacker's vital area and your shots are all hitting accurately inside that area, all your rounds are contributing their statistical maximum to causing his incapacitation. If you take the time and expend the energy to cluster your rounds closer together, none of those bullets is likely to be doing a better job than the others — but the time factor means you'll take longer to make the first shot, or be able to shoot fewer follow-up shots in any given amount of time.

When dealing with an attacker, all you're doing is giving him your time to hurt you or someone else.

*Keep the goal in mind*

The shots you fire affect your attacker's ability to carry out his attack. Wouldn't it be better to make your shots happen sooner rather than later? Wouldn't it be better to shoot faster and accept a little less artificial precision as long as you're still hitting in the area that is likely to result in incapacitation? I think it is!

At the same time, inaccurate shots waste your time, ammunition, and effort. If your shot lands outside the area of precision you've recognized, it may damage the attacker but it doesn't do as much to bring about his incapacitation as the shot that lands inside the recognized vital area does. You're better off exerting effort — taking a little extra time to apply your skill — to bring your shot into the area of precision you've recognized so it will stop the attack more reliably.

Here's where training and practice come in: If you don't *recognize* the level of precision the target requires, you won't apply the level of skill needed to deliver it, and your rounds won't have their maximum effect. Shots that don't contribute their maximum to stopping your attacker waste your time, energy, and available ammunition — they are inefficient. Being able to recognize the level of precision and then deliver it *is* being efficient and should be your objective.

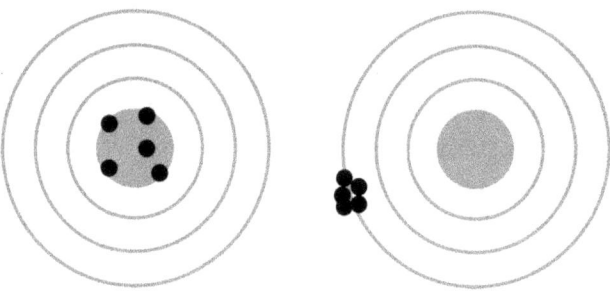

*Target on left is accurate but not particularly precise. Target on right is very precise but not accurate.*

### Shooting is always a tradeoff

In the mid-1950s a hunting expert named Francis Sell wrote a little book called "Small Game Hunting", in which he outlined a concept he called "trading time for accuracy". While his terminology wasn't quite perfect (it's clear he meant what we know today as precision, rather than accuracy) his observation was: The greater the precision your target requires, the more time it will take you to land an accurate shot inside that area.

As it happens, his ideas apply to all shooting — not just hunting.

It's also fair to say that what he wrote wasn't really a revelation; anyone with nearly any amount of shooting experience knows almost intuitively that the more difficult the shot, the more carefully you'll probably shoot. Shooting carefully means exerting more control over yourself and your rifle to accurately hit the recognized area of precision. More control takes more time, and accepting that simple equation is key to shooting well.

Why might you take more time to shoot? Perhaps because you need to make a little more effort in aligning your sights on a smaller or more distant target; because you need a more stable shooting position for a target of that size at that distance; or because the lighting conditions or the amount of precipitation coming down or some other environmental variable makes it harder to both see the target and control your rifle.

Whatever the circumstances, the more carefully you need to shoot the more time it will take you to fire the first (and each subsequent) round.

If you've been shooting for any length of time, you've been making use of this concept without really thinking about it. When faced with a more difficult shot you've probably buckled down, been more careful, and accepted that you were going to spend more time getting an accurate hit on the target. That's the whole concept in a nutshell.

All shooting, including defensive rifle shooting, comes down to trading time for precision. At its simplest, it means an increase in precision necessitates a corresponding increase in your use of skill, which in turn results in an increase in the time taken to make the shot. On the other hand, shortening the time to make a shot, whether it's the first or a followup shot, usually results in a decrease in achievable precision. There's more to it, but the relationship between time and precision is the key.

As I've already pointed out, this isn't a new concept. If you've been shooting much, you already have an intuitive — if incomplete — grasp of the concept. It's not something I made up for this book, and it isn't just for target shooting.

Your own personal time versus precision tradeoff will change with a host of variables: the size of the target, the distance to the target, whether it's bright or dark, how fatigued you are, the shooting position you're forced to adopt, the temperature, how much coffee you've had, what kind of clothing you're wearing, and more.

The tradeoff you make in any given situation will be different than someone else's in the same situation, and will change from day to day. It will even change over the length of a training or practice session as your fatigue level increases.

In the beginning you'll make this tradeoff consciously; you'll decide to take more time to make a more difficult shot. As you gain experience, making that tradeoff happens imperceptibly as your brain recognizes that it's done this thing before and knows exactly how much time to take to reach a specific level of precision. Getting to the point that you know, without needing to think, what you need to do for any given combination of target and environmental variable is why you practice your shooting skills under a wide range of conditions.

### Remember: the target dictates precision

As I pointed out earlier, your target dictates the precision you need to deliver. On a paper target, the precision is dictated by the markings; in defensive shooting, that area is one you need to figure out — and quickly.

Your attacker's physiology and position relative to you dictate the precision needed, but intervening obstacles — such as other people, or objects he's hiding behind or that are between you and him —factor into that area as well. In all cases, it falls to you to recognize the precision needed and apply the amount of your skill necessary to deliver that level of precision.

*Skill determines accuracy*

On the other hand, it's your skill — or more precisely, your *use* of your available skill — that causes your shots to land inside the target area. Your skill determines whether or not you're accurate.

You'll likely always experience some difference between where you intend the shot to go and where it actually does, and controlling that difference is how accuracy is achieved. Minimizing that difference means applying more control over your rifle, which comes is what your skill entails.

Controlling that difference takes both time and effort on your part. A large target area very close to you requires less control than a smaller target that is farther away. As more precision is needed, you must apply more control, which takes more time.

Back to recognition: You practice to associate in your mind a given level of control with what the target is dictating. When you need to make the shot, your brain recalls how much control you need to apply (and how to apply it). When you've done that, you've used your skill to make the shot.

## Every shot is a tradeoff

Many people think that a time-versus-precision tradeoff refers to how fast you can pull the trigger in rapid succession. It's actually concerned with and applies to the first shot you fire just as much as (perhaps more than) every other shot.

*The all-important first shot*

That first shot is your *best opportunity* to affect the attacker's ability to hurt you or the life you're protecting. Once the first round is fired, the situation deteriorates; people (and animals) start moving, and the scene becomes more chaotic. Should that first shot miss, landing an accurate second shot becomes more difficult. Even if it hits exactly where you intended it to, you might need to shoot again if it didn't have the expected effect or if there is more than one attacker.

Once you've made the decision to shoot, based on what's happening in front of your eyes, there is still a lot you need to do. If the rifle doesn't already have a round chambered, you need to quickly put it into a condition where it's ready to shoot. You need to assess what level of precision the target requires of you and what shooting position you need to use to deliver that level of precision.

Regardless of your selected shooting position, the rifle has to get onto your shoulder and in contact with your cheek, and the safety, if the rifle is so equipped, has to be turned off. Then the actual act of shooting commences as you align the sights, whether iron or optical, on the target, your finger touches the trigger, and finally you press the trigger to the rear without disturbing the gun's alignment on target.

As I said, it's a lot to do. Once you've decided to shoot, all those things probably need to happen very quickly. Your application of skill, particularly where sight alignment and trigger press are concerned, determines whether you make the shot.

*How quickly should you shoot again?*

You're responsible for every bullet that comes out of your gun, and if that bullet is fired recklessly or inappropriately, the consequences can be harsh. As a responsible gun owner and shooter, it's up to you to shoot when it's necessary and to stop shooting when the threat to lives has ended.

That's why I'm a firm believer that you shouldn't be shooting faster than you can assess and make decisions. Defensive shooting, whether the first round or a subsequent round, should never be a reflexive action. It should be a deliberate decision to an articulable threat. Deliberate doesn't necessarily mean slow. It means you must have a reason to shoot — and you must know what that reason is.

What if you need to shoot more than once, especially on the same target? How fast can you assess the situation and shoot again?

The answer is: as soon as you recognize that you need to shoot again. Shoot fast enough that you're not wasting time your attacker can use to his advantage, but not so fast that you can't make the decision to stop shooting.

That's actually pretty fast, but many people can physically shoot faster than they can observe and decide. In my classes, I'd say most students can physically shoot much more rapidly than they can observe and make decision.

Most defensive rifle courses focus on the physical act of shooting, training their students to constantly reduce their split times (the time between successive shots). The implicit lesson is that you don't have time to think about it, and that making decisions takes too long. I would disagree with that contention.

*A lesson from competition*

Back in the days when I shot handguns in competition, my favorite sport was Steel Challenge-type* courses, where the objective was to shoot five steel targets as quickly as possible. One of the five targets is usually smaller and is called the "stop plate."

The rules are simple: You have to hit all four designated targets before you hit the stop plate. Once the stop plate is hit, that's the end of the shooting string. If for some reason the stop plate is hit before all the other plates, a heavy penalty is assigned for that run.

A Steel Challenge run starts with the gun in the holster and hands above the shoulders. When the buzzer sounds, the shooter draws and hits all five plates as fast as he or she can.

How fast is that? A reasonably skilled shooter on "Smoke-n-Hope," one of the faster stages, can draw and hit all five targets in about 2.5 seconds. A really good shooter takes significantly less than two seconds. All the time, he or she has to be assessing: "Did I hit that target? Do I need to shoot it again? Can I go on to the next target?"

I can remember more than one instance when I fired at the stop plate, recognized that I missed, and made the decision to shoot again — all, according to the timer, in about a quarter-second. In other words, you have plenty of time to make the decision to shoot again if you need to. There's little justification for, or value in, pulling the trigger as quickly as you possibly can.

*Practice for confidence*

Your confidence in your own abilities is a big part of this equation. Confidence is the correlation between what you *think* you can do and what you really can do. Confidence comes from your training and practice, which is why training and practicing under realistic conditions (recognizing varying levels of precision) are so important.

If your skills and your confidence in those skills are correctly linked, you'll always be able to shoot as fast as you can assess and make decisions. You'll apply the correct amount of control over your gun to get the hits you need, and actually get them.

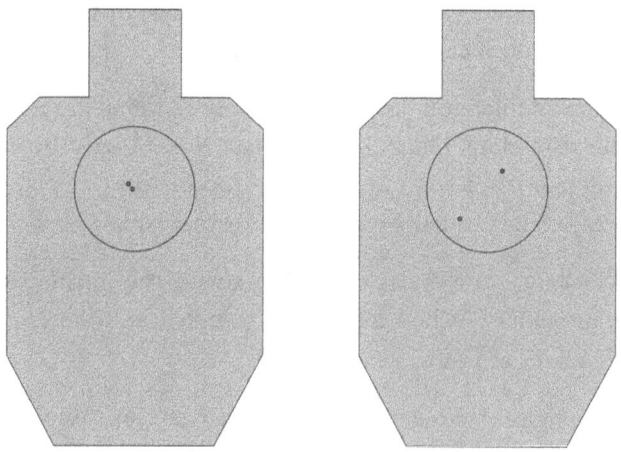

*Shooting to a greater degree of precision than the target requires, as on the left,*

*takes more effort and application of skill — which takes more time. Target on right shows an understanding of the balance of speed and precision: applying enough control to shoot to the level of skill the target requires, but no more.*

---

\* - https://en.wikipedia.org/wiki/Steel_Challenge

*Chapter Fourteen*
# AIMING CONCEPTS

When faced with a threat, particularly a lethal threat, it's natural for the body to marshal all its resources to defeating that threat. As a result, the body has some specific and largely predictable reactions when faced with a potential loss of life.

One of the more important is the tendency to focus on the threat you're facing. This is part of the brain's desire to know as much about what's trying to kill it as possible. The closer or more immediate the threat, the greater the tendency to want to focus on that threat to gather information. At least initially, your vision is likely to be locked onto the threat, whether it be human or animal.

### Effect on your sights

This normal, natural tendency plays very well with optical and electro-optical sighting devices, which place the reticle (aiming point or device) in the same plane as the target. Using a sighting system allows you to keep that very natural threat focus, which in turn makes using those systems under stress easier.

This is why I heartily recommend a low-power (1-4X or so) scope or red-dot optic for a perimeter defense rifle. Their design, with the aiming reticle in the same focus plane as the target, simplifies using the rifle against a threat. You just keep your focus on the target, where it wants to be anyhow, place the dot or crosshairs on the spot you want to shoot, and press the trigger. It doesn't matter how close or far away the target is — your technique remains the same. It's as close to "point and click" as shooting ever gets.

But if you're using conventional (iron or open) sights, you have more to consider. Most sight use is based on the idea of focusing on the front sight and allowing the target (threat) to blur. This is counter to your natural threat reactions, which want you to focus on the thing that's attacking. It's also counter to the idea of assessing your threat before, during, and after you shoot.

Without optical aids, you can only keep one thing in focus at a time: the threat, your front sight, or your rear sight. Something is going to be sharp and everything else is going to be blurry, and without lenses in between, you can't change that.

But you can adjust your technique to something that works better with your natural tendency to focus on the threat.

### Threat-centered iron-sight technique

Believe it or not, you actually can shoot a rifle fairly accurately even when your focus is locked on the target. This runs counter to everything I was ever taught, and I suspect counter to everything you were taught, but it's true.

Two kinds of deviation can occur with iron sights. First is the deviation caused by poor front/rear sight alignment. This is known as a *superposition* error: the error encountered when two items are out of proper alignment.

The second type of deviation is a *superimposition* error, which we call a sight-picture error: the improper placement on the target of properly aligned sights.

Traditional rifle teaching says that to hit a target with iron sights, you must focus on the front sight to the exclusion of all else. Because the human eye can only focus in one plane at a time, that means the rear sight and — most importantly — the target are both out of focus.

The standard front-sight focus sacrifices some superimposition error in order to reduce the superposition error. In other words, it trades off sight picture (because it's hard to judge exactly where to place your sights, and thus where the bullet will hit, on a blurry target) in order to get better sight alignment.

The reality, though, is that the sights still work as long as *something* is in focus. It can be the front sight or the target; if either element is in focus, the sights can be used to align the gun. If your vision is focused on the threat, as it's likely to be if you're facing something or someone who poses a direct danger to your life, you can still use your iron sights. All you need to do is keep your focus on the target.

*Front sight (left) versus target/threat focus (right)*

With a target focus, you make the tradeoff in the other direction: You sacrifice sight alignment (superposition error) to get better sight picture (superimposition error). As it happens, they're often about the same amount, and in many cases trading one for the other produces negligible change in performance.

Target focus works best with front sights that have a round bead, as opposed to those with straight sides and a flat top. Even though your sights are blurred, you can still align them and then place them on the sharp target. While you'll sacrifice some deviation in alignment, it will be compensated by better placement on target. The errors will, for most people at most plausible defensive distances, cancel out.

The key is to keep your focus on the target but slightly shift your attention to aligning the sights, blurred though they may be. Think of looking through the sights, not at them.

This technique is made easier with ghost ring or peep sights, but can be successfully accomplished with standard open sights*. Once aligned, you can take advantage of the sharp target for more precise placement.

This target focus method is extremely fast, although people trained in the traditional hard front-sight focus method often have trouble adjusting. My own adjustment period was motivated by the aging process, as I couldn't see the sights without using bifocals — which, of course, are nearly impossible to employ with a rifle.

Again, the beauty of the optical sight is you don't need to choose between the two deviation errors. The optical sight reduces both superposition and superimposition errors to practically zero**, making precision shooting far easier and faster.

If you wear corrective lenses, as I do, and are limited to iron sights, you may find this threat-centered approach allows you to make accurate shots on surprisingly small targets at longer distances. It may never be as precise for you as a traditional sight focus, but it's usable when the traditional method might not be. Don't take my word for it, though: Practice this technique at the range, at plausible defensive distances, and find out if it's a workable solution for you.

## Elevation and windage

Correcting for bullet drop and wind drift is a big part of long distance and target shooting, but it isn't a concern in perimeter defense except in rare cases.

At the ranges we're considering, bullet drop for most rifle calibers won't be a significant issue. An inch or so of bullet drop isn't a major concern with any predatory creature, two legged or four, against which shooting is a reasonable and lawful response.

The only exceptions to this rule are low-powered rounds like the .22 Long Rifle (which shouldn't be used against most threats beyond about 25 yards) and heavy, low-velocity cartridges like the old .45-70. (Sighted in for zero at 100 yards, this round will drop nearly four inches at 150 yards. Add just 10 yards, to 160, and it drops over five inches!)

If you're using such a round for your perimeter defense rifle, you'll need to become adept at judging your distance to target and making adjustments in your aim point to compensate. Very carefully selecting your zero range is also important to maximize your effective point-blank shooting distance.

*Windage corrections*

Compensating for the effects of wind aren't much of a concern at the relatively modest distances we're considering for perimeter defense. However, some very light bullets (such as the 55-grain loads in the .223/5.56) can be affected by strong gusty winds. A sudden 20mph gust at right angles to you at the moment you decide to fire might push your bullet off by nearly two inches.

Under those conditions, it may be prudent to add a little "Kentucky windage" to your aim. This is shooting slang for aiming slightly to the side to compensate for the wind. Keep the following in mind:

- Unless you're shooting in a raging storm, most winds will not affect most bullets enough to worry about at the moderate distances of perimeter defense.
- In general, the lighter the bullet, the more likely you are to need to compensate for wind.

- Winds at right angles will affect your bullet's path the most. If the wind is roughly in line with your line of sight, it won't affect your bullet very much (if at all).

If you live in an area with frequent winds and you choose a lightweight round like the .223/5.56, you may need to learn to aim one to two inches into the direction of the wind, depending on the strength (speed) and at what angle it arrives. It's very much a subjective and spur-of-the-moment call that illustrates the need for practice under the conditions you expect to use your defensive rifle.

Picking the right bullet can help reduce the drift in windy conditions. Again using the .223/5.56 cartridge as an example, the heavier 77-grain bullets move a little less in the wind than do the lighter and more common 55-grain bullets. If you live in a windy area, picking your load for its wind resistance may be a good idea.

You can get wind-drift information for most cartridges and bullets from the manufacturer's website. Some ballistic calculators also have pre-programmed information for many factory loads, which allows you to compare across manufacturers.

*Estimating your correction*

One of the great things about the modern age is that you can have interactive tools with you on the range to help you estimate things like windage corrections (and zero distances). Ballistics apps are available for just about every smartphone and tablet. They let you pick your cartridge, bullet, range, wind speed, and wind direction — and then tell you what your corrections need to be.

I want to emphasize that these aren't intended to be used in the heat and chaos of an actual incident, but rather to help you learn and internalize the information during your shooting practice. If you practice at the distances you're likely to need to shoot, and you practice realistically (not sitting down on a bench, but shooting from actual field positions), ballistics apps can be great learning aids.

\* - *Target shooters with iron sights almost invariably use a rear peep sight with an extremely small aperture (opening). This acts much like the diaphragm in a camera lens: As the peep gets smaller in diameter, the depth of field increases. While the target never appears sharp even with a small peep, it does get less blurry and therefore decreases the superimposition error to a great degree. The problem with this approach is that those very tiny apertures aren't fast to use, and if the available light decreases, they can become nearly impossible to use. My .22 target rifle is equipped with such a peep sight, and it's great on a sunny day, but on a gray cloudy day becomes much less usable.*

\*\* - *On an absolute basis, while sight alignment is no longer an issue with the optical sights, the sight picture may be. The greater the magnification of the sight, the less superimposition deviation you'll experience, but the slower the sight will be to use and the more dependent you'll be on your stability. A 24-power scope is great if the rifle is sitting on a concrete shooting bench, but darn near impossible to use from a standing position because it magnifies every little muscle tremor (even your heartbeat). It's also useless if the target is within 25 yards or so.*

## Chapter Fifteen
# TRIGGER CONTROL

Trigger control in perimeter defense more closely resembles that of combat than of target shooting. In addition to the body's normal physiological threat responses, you'll likely need to deal with some fatigue and shortness of breath, which come from the need to go to the rifle and then bring the rifle to the scene.

Again, one of the salient characteristics of perimeter defense is that you need to retrieve the rifle. This means you may have to run to your house (or truck, or wherever the rifle is staged or stored), get the rifle, then run back to where you can actually use the rifle. Even if you're in very good shape, this is going to result in a certain amount of physical fatigue.

That fatigue — muscle weakness or trembling, shortness of breath, etc. — will affect how you operate your rifle. The nice, calm trigger press taught in most target-shooting or hunting courses may become nearly impossible, while you're still left with the need to make a precision shot at distance.

Trigger control in perimeter defense hinges on your ability to precisely manipulate your finger under the very conditions that make it difficult to do so.

**Trigger weight**

A few years ago, I bought a new AR-15 from a reputable manufacturer. It's a nice rifle and has served me well, but it came with a trigger that I considered horrendous for the job of self-defense.

The trigger, which the company referred to as a "two-stage match trigger," broke at just about three pounds. It was crisp, predictable, and very nice in the conventional target-shooting sense. It was one of the best triggers I'd felt on an AR-15 up to that time.

It was also exactly what I didn't want for a rifle that would likely be used in a stressful situation, because my experience told me the weight of that trigger was well below the force my finger would be able to modulate after even a small amount of fatigue.

I promptly switched out the trigger package for a regular old military-style trigger, which requires about six pounds to fire. Several of my friends thought I was crazy to give up the nicer trigger, but none of them had my experience using a rifle to defend themselves or their homesteads.

I've found a single-stage trigger of between five and six pounds to be ideal for defensive purposes. It's light enough that it doesn't really affect my ability to place precision shots at plausible perimeter defense distances, but not so light that I might fire a round inadvertently under the diminished tactile sensitivity that usually accompanies stress and/or fatigue.

For defensive use, I recommend you not replace your stock trigger (or have any work done to the trigger) unless it's extremely light or extremely heavy. Most rifles, even the less expensive models, usually come with triggers that are eminently suitable for defensive use — though there are exceptions. The most common exceptions I can think of are some bullpup rifles, which are infamous for their heavy trigger weights.*

## Trigger technique

Trigger technique in target shooting is somewhat different than it is in defensive shooting. In defensive shooting, you may need to deal with being tired, out of breath, scared, trembling, or perhaps all at the same time. It's for this reason I don't recommend light, target-style triggers, and also why I recommend a trigger technique that still lets you make accurate shots under these conditions.

First, place your finger on the trigger so the trigger lands somewhere between the middle of the pad and the first joint. The heavier the trigger on your rifle, the closer to (or even on) the joint it should be placed.

This trigger position gives better control under stress (when tactile sensation is likely to be reduced) and, at the same time, optimum leverage.

*The ideal trigger press*

It's often been said that for accurate shooting, the trigger break (the point at which it releases the firing pin and ignites the round) should come as a "surprise." This is not how defensive shooting should be done. You need to know exactly when the trigger breaks, and you're the one who decides at what instant it happens.

Gone is the slow trigger press where the finger applies controlled and increasing pressure on the trigger until the surprise break. Instead, your trigger control needs to be focused on pressing the trigger quickly without disturbing the alignment of your sights on target.

As you bring your rifle to your shoulder, your trigger finger should touch the trigger; that is, it should land on the trigger face in the correct spot, ready to fire the shot when you decide it needs to be fired.

For rifles with two-stage triggers or those with trigger safeties (such as on the Savage Accu-Trigger models), touching the trigger actually depresses the trigger (or the safety). That's perfectly fine. It's how those trigger mechanisms are designed to work. If you have a two-stage trigger, the pressure of your finger touching the trigger face should cause it to depress to the second stage point, where the trigger weight is noticeably higher and the finger naturally stops.

When the decision to fire is made, the trigger is pressed straight back. The key is to rapidly increase the pressure on your trigger finger so it overcomes the weight of the trigger's springs and the gun fires. The shot should break exactly when you want it to.

This action is much faster than target shooters (or even hunters) are used to. Again, the trigger breaks when *you* want it to, without hesitation or waiting. The only way this happens is if your trigger finger moves quickly, but not spasmodically or roughly, when needed. It's not a jerk, but it is swift.

### *The expedient trigger press*

There are conditions under which even the small pause between touching the trigger and pressing it to fire the shot isn't desired; when it's necessary to accept a small reduction in precision for a small increase in speed. When the shot needs to happen immediately, even a tiny extra amount of time seems like an eternity.

If, for instance, your target is quite close (in rifle terms) and the precision of the ideal trigger press isn't needed — but speed certainly is — you may need to forego the action of first touching the trigger. Under such conditions, the trigger press becomes part of the shouldering process. This is a major component of what used to be called "snap shooting."

As the rifle comes to a horizontal position (from whatever starting point) and becomes roughly indexed on target, the safety is disengaged. As the butt is pulled toward the shoulder, the trigger finger is allowed to touch the trigger. As the butt contacts the shoulder and aim on target is confirmed through the sights, the trigger finger swiftly and smoothly moves the trigger through both the take-up and sear release in one continuous motion. The effect is reminiscent of shooting a double-action revolver quickly.

Conscious attention should be paid to the follow-through after a rapid shot, as it's quite easy to jerk the muzzle off target and actually affect the path of the bullet if the trigger finger releases pressure as quickly as it applied it.

*Follow-through*

One common issue I see with students in my perimeter defense Rifle course is when their trigger finger causes the barrel to deviate slightly from aim as the bullet leaves the barrel. This sounds impossible, but just about any rifle or shotgun coach can verify that it happens.

While it can be caused by poor trigger press, that's usually found easily because it can be seen through the sights or scope. The other cause isn't as easily diagnosed: poor follow-through.

Many people want to learn to shoot their rifle rapidly — multiple rounds in a very short time, like competition or "tactical" shooters do. This requires the shooter to reset the trigger at almost the instant the shot is fired. The only way to do that is to relax the trigger finger so it moves forward and allows the trigger to reset.

The problem is the muscles in the forearm. The *flexor digitorum superficialis* controls the flexing of the trigger finger. When that muscle relaxes, the extrinsic *extensor* muscles on the opposite side pull the finger back to its starting position. This combined action of two large muscles often causes the wrist to rotate just a bit, which can cause the muzzle to move and the shot to land off of the aiming point — sometimes enough to cause a miss.

A very easy way to cure this problem is to pay attention to follow-through. If you've played golf, tennis, or baseball, you're no doubt already familiar with the need for proper follow-through — although this application is a bit different.

In rifle shooting, follow-through means to pause the trigger finger momentarily when the shot fires. As the shot breaks, your trigger finger holds the trigger in the fired position for a half-second or so. Some instructors say to "trap the trigger with your finger."

In the beginning stages, I've found it helpful to learn correct follow-through by exaggerating the trapping motion. Make your pause deliberate: Hold the trigger for a full second before releasing (resetting) it. You want the pause to be long enough so that when you allow the trigger to reset, you can hear the distinct "click" it makes.

After you see the effect on your shooting and ingrain the concept, the duration of the follow-through can be allowed to naturally shorten.

Once you've learned the concept, you'll likely discover that, even when shooting very rapidly, there's always a slight pause for follow-through at the conclusion of each shot.

While this problem usually shows up with semiautomatic rifles, those shooting manually operated repeaters like the lever-action and bolt-action aren't immune to the problem. This is particularly true if they learned to shoot with a pistol or revolver, where rapid fire is virtually always part of the curriculum. The same prescription will improve shooting on those rifles, too. The only difference is that you won't feel the trigger "click" as it resets, because the reset is done by operating the bolt or lever.

*Dealing with the very heavy trigger*

As I've said, most rifles come with triggers that are very usable for self-defense. In fact, most rifles today come with triggers that just a decade or so ago would have been considered excellent.

But a few rifles — usually those with military history or design — have triggers that are quite heavy. Earlier I singled out the bullpup rifle as typically heavier than average, though they're certainly not the only ones.

Simply stated, the heavier the trigger, the harder it is for most people to place precision shots at longer distances. It's hard to apply enough force to move the trigger without disturbing the rifle's alignment on target.

If you have such a rifle, proper technique will allow you to shoot better than most people think possible — even with triggers whose weights are on the extreme end of the scale.

Start by placing your first (*distal interphalangeal*) finger joint on the trigger. Traditional marksmanship always preaches to use the pad of your finger to press the trigger, but that won't give you the leverage and control you need for a very heavy trigger. Shifting to the first joint instead of the pad will.

Some instructors refer to this position as the "power crease," because it allows you to produce tremendous force yet keep it under control. If you're a seasoned rifle shooter, especially if you were trained in conventional competitive shooting techniques, this is going to seem very foreign to you. (If you're an avid handgun shooter, particularly if you shoot double-action revolvers, it will seem right at home.)

Your shooting hand grasp is also important. You'll be applying a lot of force to the trigger, and that force needs to be properly directed yet controlled. Uncontrolled force is what steers the gun out of alignment with the target.

If your rifle has a pistol-type grip, make sure your hand is in a position where the line of force from your finger is traveling as close to straight back, to the point the stock contacts your shoulder, as possible. Then position your hand on the grip so your palm is on that line of force.

If you're using a conventionally stocked rifle, the force from your trigger finger should come naturally toward your palm. It's best to have your thumb pointing forward and just to the side of the centerline of the stock, as opposed to being thrown over the opposite side. This puts the pad at the base of the thumb (the *thenar eminence*, for those into anatomy) directly opposite the line of force from the trigger finger, and prevents the slight rolling of the rifle that sometimes occurs when the thumb is placed over the top.

A heavy trigger requires a much firmer grasp than a lighter trigger does; it's the only way to counter the force your trigger finger is exerting. Grasp the rifle very firmly, making sure that all the fingers of your hand are engaged (contributing to the grasp). As your trigger finger applies more pressure, the other fingers on that hand will want to flex sympathetically. The tighter they already are, the less they can flex and drive the rifle off target.

When your finger is in the proper position and you have a proper grasp, apply rapidly increasing pressure on the trigger. Increase the amount of force quickly until you overcome the weight of the trigger and the gun fires.

Note that I'm not saying to "grab" or jerk the trigger; this should not be a spasmodic movement. Think of the trigger as a car's accelerator pedal, and you need to get up to speed to merge into highway traffic on a wet road. Rather than instantly mashing the pedal to the floor and spinning your wheels, you instead smoothly yet swiftly push the pedal down until you're at maximum acceleration. Do this with a heavy trigger and you'll find your shooting precision increasing.

---

*\* - Many people attribute heavy bullpup triggers to the linkage required to fire the rifle, but the reality is that linkages aren't the problem. The issue stems from the fact that most of them have been designed for military use and fully automatic fire, and for users who might be wearing heavy gloves while shooting. Knowing their context of use, you can better appreciate the need for a trigger that is very difficult to trip accidentally.*

*Chapter Sixteen*

# SHOOTING POSITIONS

At its core, perimeter defense is about moving with the rifle into a place where you may have to employ it against a threat. Because the goal is always to stop a threat, and because threat scenarios requiring that level of force evolve rapidly, it may be necessary to shoot from a hastily acquired position.

At the same time, it's important to remember that you're always balancing how fast you can shoot and the degree of precision to which you can shoot. The fastest-to-acquire shooting position is almost always going to produce the lowest possible precision — and that is, in fact, exactly what happens. The more stable the shooting position, the greater the precision you can achieve, but the more time you'll take getting into that position.

No one position is ideal for every shooting situation. Instead, you'll decide your shooting position based on not just the speed/precision equation, but also taking into account the environmental variables. Some conditions simply won't allow certain shooting positions, and the more stable any given shooting position is, the more subject it is to environmental restrictions.

Sometimes, being able to get *out* of your shooting position quickly is as important as being able to get into it quickly. If you're dealing with a human attacker, your mobility (to seek cover, for example) may be a very important component of your defensive response. If you need to move quickly, some shooting positions are going to be better than others.

Let's look at the most commonly used shooting positions and their application in perimeter defense.

## Standing

Standing without any form of support is often referred to as "off-hand" shooting. It's also the primary shooting position in perimeter defense because of its speed. Standing is the fastest position to acquire: All you need to do is stop moving and bring the rifle to your shoulder.

At the same time, standing is the least stable shooting position and therefore has the least potential for precision. The smaller the target or the greater the distance, the less usable the standing position becomes.

The standing position is also more affected by fatigue, excitement, and exhaustion than other shooting positions. If you're out of breath because you had to run a distance to retrieve your rifle (or because of the stress of the incident), the standing position is going to be the most difficult from which to shoot.

*The Base*

The standing position should be thought of as two somewhat independent parts: the base, from the hips down, and the turret, from the hips up. Each plays an important role.

The base is your interface with the world, and at the same time is at the mercy of the world. Where your feet end up, for example, is dependent on the terrain: You may be on a slope, or one foot may be on a different surface than the other. Sometimes you can quickly choose a more advantageous foot position, but when time is short, that may not be an option and you'll be forced to shoot from whatever position you find yourself in.

For this reason, you should start with a natural, balanced foot position, which I refer to as the "neutral" position. If the incident forces you into an extreme foot placement, it's easier to adapt from neutral than if you're accustomed to the opposite extreme.

Let me give you an example: I've seen more than a few students who learned to shoot from a very exaggerated foot position (which they were told would help them "control recoil"), and when circumstances required them to shoot from in a situation where their foot positions were reversed, they literally could not hit the target.

But from a neutral position, any extreme is closer to what you're used to. If you learn to shoot from a neutral foot placement, and the incident forces your feet into an exaggerated (and even uncomfortable) placement, it's easier to adapt than if you're accustomed to something that was exaggerated in the opposite direction.

What does this natural, balanced position look like? Imagine a line drawn on the ground in front of you. Your feet are approximately shoulder-width apart, giving you good lateral stability without fatigue. Your strong-hand foot may naturally assume a position slightly behind the line, while your weak-side foot is on or perhaps slightly ahead of the line. The offset shouldn't be exaggerated and should always feel comfortable.

Your knees should be unlocked; that is, they should have a little bit of movement potential left both forward and backward. If you bring your knees all the way back, to the point that they can't go any farther, they're said to be "locked." That's not the most stable or flexible position: Let them move forward a bit, so they have some flex. This is where your muscles can work naturally and most efficiently to stabilize your body, which is important to holding the rifle steady.

*The Turret*

The turret, your upper body, can rotate independently of the base. Its position relative to the target will depend on your build and the dimensions of the rifle you're shooting. If you have long arms and/or a shorter rifle stock, your torso will be facing the threat more than if you have a longer stock or shorter arms.

If your base has by necessity ended up in a very odd position, your turret may have to rotate considerably to orient to the threat and properly align (aim) the rifle. You can experiment with this anywhere and without a rifle: Stand in a normal shooting position and take note of where your chest is relative to your head. Now, rotate your base — take a step back with your strong-side foot, as if you were going to turn around. Keep your head and chest oriented to the target. Now do the opposite (move your weak-side foot instead). See how your torso can, within limits, keep an imaginary rifle on target?

The butt of the rifle should be placed inside of your shoulder, in what's called "the pocket." To find the right place, do this test: Using your fingers, reach over and touch the shoulder of your opposite arm. You should be able to feel the socket and, as you move your fingers toward the center of your body, you'll feel a depression where your collarbone curves to meet the shoulder socket. That's the pocket, and it's where you can effectively control the rifle's recoil without injury.

Some instructors will tell you to move the butt more toward the center of your body, placing it just below (or even on) the collarbone. This idea comes from the military close-quarter-battle (CQB) world, where everyone wears body armor that pads the collarbone and prevents injury. In the un-armored private sector, you can make this work with the gentle recoil of the AR-15 chambered in .223/5.56, but you'll find it quite painful for any cartridge that generates substantially greater recoil.

Vertical positioning of the butt is important as well. Too low on the shoulder, and you'll need to crane your neck unnecessarily to get your cheek on the buttstock. Too high, and you'll concentrate the recoil forces into a small point. A good starting point is to place the top of the butt just above your collarbone; some rifles, like the AR-15, can be placed a little higher. Experiment to find your best fit.

For comfort and consistency, I shoot all rifles from the "pocket" and recommend you do the same. I've fired as many as 800 rounds of .308 Winchester rifle ammunition over a two-day period in training, all from the pocket, without issue. I couldn't have done this had the rifle's butt been placed anywhere else.

Your shooting hand should be on the control point, where it can operate (at a minimum) the trigger and safety. If you're using a rifle with a pistol grip, like the AR-15, the shooting hand should be as high on the pistol grip as possible to maximize the trigger-finger position. If your rifle has a conventional stock, such as most bolt-actions and lever-actions, the shooting-hand position should be determined by how easily you can reach the trigger with the pad of your trigger finger.

*Elbow up or down?*

It used to be taught (and in some places may still be) that the shooting-hand elbow be raised so the arm was parallel to the ground.

Back in the days when everyone used a bolt-action rifle, this position had some merit. The raised elbow tended to delineate the shoulder pocket more clearly, leading to consistent positioning, and forced the rifle inward and firmly against the cheek. Some shooters may also have found that it made bolt manipulation easier.

The raised elbow position doesn't work nearly as well with a pistol-gripped rifle, as it tends to twist the wrist unnaturally, making it more difficult to achieve a trigger press that is in line with the rifle. With the ascendency of the pistol-gripped AR-15 (and others) over the decades, the preference has turned to having the shooting elbow down.

This elbow position is more comfortable and less fatiguing, and having the elbow down makes it much easier to swing to follow a moving target. It's also more consistent with the placement of the elbow in every other shooting stance. For these reasons, most instructors today teach elbow down.

There is a difference, however, between elbow-down and having the elbow tucked in. The elbow should be in a natural position. Tucking it in does little good but, like having the elbow artificially raised, fatigues the arm sooner.

A tucked-in elbow when shooting many rounds in rapid fire has some value, but the difference is minimal and really not a factor in realistic defensive scenarios.

*Pay attention to the thumb*

With conventionally stocked rifles (such as lever- and bolt-actions), I recommend your shooting thumb not be draped or curled over the stock. Instead, the thumb should be pointed in the direction of the muzzle and sit naturally to the side of an imaginary line running parallel to the barrel. This will position your shooting hand to operate the bolt or lever most efficiently without unduly disturbing the gun's aim.

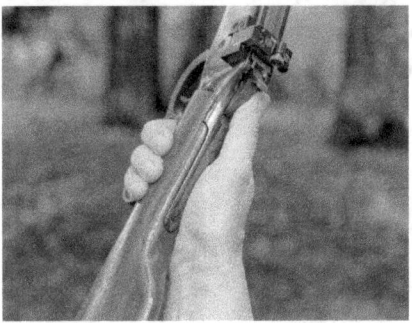

*Less desirable thumb placement (top) and optimal thumb placement (bottom) on a conventionally-stocked rifle.*

## Squatting

This position isn't found in many rifle shooting texts, particularly the older ones, but it has great application in the world of defensive rifle shooting. Sometimes referred to as "rice paddy prone," it's an adaptation of a shooting position frequently encountered by our troops in the various Southeast Asia wars.

It has the advantage of being, with a little practice, almost as fast to acquire as standing. It's also very fast to move from, as all you need to do is stand up. At the same time, it's substantially more stable than standing — at least for the first shot. It keeps all your body parts off the ground, which means you don't get wet or risk the possibility of injury from debris or rough surfaces.

For all its attributes, it's not a position everyone can use, as it relies to a great degree on physical flexibility. As I've aged, I've gotten less proficient with this position (though I admit a bit of a middle-age bulge is largely responsible). I also find it somewhat fatiguing, though people in other countries appear to be able to maintain this position for long periods of time while working.

A proper squatting position requires that both feet be flat on the ground. The exact placement of the feet is highly individualistic. Experiment to find what works best for you as you get into the position.

With your feet flat on the ground, just squat as tightly and as low as you can. Bring your derriere down close to the backs of your calves and lean your upper body forward to balance. The key is to lean forward from your ankles. Having a rifle in your hands as you do this will help, as the extra forward weight makes balancing easier.

Those who haven't grown up with this position often have trouble with balance, as it initially feels as though you're going to topple over backwards. None of my students ever has, and neither have I, but it is a little disconcerting and requires repetition to build the familiarity that leads to confidence.

To get into a shooting position, place the elbows on the protruding knees. Exactly where the elbows end up depends on your flexibility. If you're tightly tucked in, which is ideal, your knees will actually be on the backs of your upper arm or on the lower end of your tricep muscles.

Because of the off-center placement of the rifle on the torso, rifle shooting stances usually end up at an angle, or "bladed," to the target. In the standing position, you have the ability to twist (traverse) your torso to bring your sights on the target regardless of where your feet are. The squatting position affords you only a tiny amount of lateral movement, so your feet need to be placed fairly well to begin with.

Most people end up at about 20 degrees to the target, again depending on individual physiology, with the strong-side foot in a trailing position relative to the other foot. You'll need to practice a bit to find out where your feet need to be placed to bring your rifle comfortably on target. The goal is to be on target for windage without any muscle engagement or strain.

I've found that clothing choice has a significant influence on how easy it is to get into the squat. Low-cut shoes afford the most ankle flexibility, while higher-cut shoes (such as hiking boots) make it harder for the ankle to bend sufficiently. The tighter the cut of your pants, the more difficult squatting will be — skinny jeans are not recommended for this position!

Once in the squatting position, you'll notice how stable it is. For many people, it is nearly as stable as sitting, while being substantially faster to get in and out of. But if you're using a heavy-recoiling rifle, it's not a position that lends itself to rapid fire. Heavy recoil definitely rocks you back on your heels, slowing down follow-up shots. I think it's a small price to pay for the squat's quickness and precision capability.

## Kneeling

The kneeling position is familiar to most shooters, especially those who have served in the military. It's a staple of most rifle shooting texts and remains one of my favorites for its overall flexibility.

Some form of the kneeling position is, for me, the most stable field position. At the same time, it's relatively fast to get into and affords a significantly greater degree of lateral movement (travel) than the squat does. It's also more comfortable than squatting, at least for me.

The downside is that it's less ideal if the ground is rough or covered with debris. In those conditions, a hastily acquired kneel can result in knee damage, and possibly severe knee injury. It's also not pleasant to practice when the ground is wet and cold, unless you're wearing rain pants.

That being said, there is no one universal kneeling position. There are numerous variations, and even I don't do it exactly the same way in every case. That's yet another advantage to the kneeling position — the ability to adapt to a wide range of environmental conditions.

### Kneeling variations

*Double kneel:* Let's start with a commonly taught kneeling position that I don't find terribly useful: the double kneel, or as some refer to it, the "penitent position." In this version, you put both knees on the ground, much as people do when they pray (hence the alternate name). You can bring your torso up for a high kneel, or tuck in for a lower position.

I'm not a fan of the double kneel because it doesn't have nearly the stability advantage of the other kneeling positions, while at the same time being slower to acquire (a great deal of care is necessary when dropping all your weight onto both knees, lest injury occur). It's also the most susceptible to injury from foreign objects on the ground.

To its credit, the double kneel does give you nearly the same lateral flexibility as standing, as you only need to twist your torso to follow a target. It's also useful if you need to shoot over a low object being used for cover.

*Artillery kneeling:* This position is named because the trailing knee gives it the appearance of an old piece of horse-drawn artillery. This version is extremely fast to get into and out of, perhaps the fastest of all kneeling variations, and gives a significant increase in stability over standing. I've used artillery kneeling myself when hunting small game, where stability and speed are both important.

To get into artillery kneeling, you start by taking a big step forward with your weak foot. Then kneel forward with your weak knee up and your strong knee trailing well behind. The strong leg is extended back to give stability, and you'll have a dramatic forward weight balance. The lower part of the strong-side leg may be straight or it might be at a slight angle to enhance lateral control.

To take advantage of the stability this position offers, place the elbow of your support arm on your knee. Depending on your build and how low you feel you need to be, place the elbow either on the fleshy area just behind the kneecap, or in front of the knee with the fleshy part of your arm (the tricep) on the kneecap. What you want to avoid is the bone-to-bone contact of the elbow joint and the kneecap, which is both unstable and uncomfortable.

To get out of artillery kneeling quickly, push backward with the weak foot, driving your center of mass more evenly to both knees, then just stand up.

One of the biggest advantages of artillery kneeling is that it's a "straight" shooting position, in that the body doesn't end up bladed to the target. Unlike the squatting position, you don't need to think about your angle to the target. This accounts for a great deal of its rapidity. Its distinct forward weight balance also makes it amenable to rapid fire with the larger calibers in a competition or class setting.

Personally, I find artillery kneeling very fatiguing; that may be its biggest disadvantage. It's not a position I'd want to hold for long periods of time, but then again its biggest virtue is speed in and out, and the assumption is that it won't be held for long.

*Textbook kneel:* I'm not sure this really has a name, but it's the kneeling position shown in most of my rifle shooting books. Hence, I'm calling it the "textbook" kneeling position. You might also refer to it as the classic kneel, for it's the kneeling position your great-grandfather probably learned when he was in the military, regardless of what country he came from.

It's a classic for a reason: It's just a good shooting position. The textbook kneel is very stable, comfortable, easy to get into (though not quite as fast as other positions), and easy to get out of. It's adaptable to a wide range of ground conditions and shooting problems, and it's fairly recoil-resistant.

To get into textbook kneel, your weak knee is up and your strong knee is down on the ground. Unlike artillery kneeling, your legs aren't splayed out dramatically; your feet are much closer together. The strong foot is placed behind the weak foot, and the strong knee is placed on the ground to form an angle if viewed from above.

The angle formed by your strong leg can be anywhere from 45 to 90 degrees, or perpendicular to the weak leg. The greater the angle, the greater your stability, but the greater the angle, the more uncomfortable or fatiguing it tends to be. In practice, I find the exact angle is determined as much by the ground conditions as by my personal preference.

The support-arm elbow is placed like it is in artillery kneeling. The biggest point to remember is to avoid placing the elbow joint on the kneecap. Any other arrangement is favorable.

The orientation of the strong-side foot is where most of the variation comes in. Some people point their toes at the ground and leave their heel up, and some take it further by resting their butt on the heel for extra stability. Some turn their foot sideways so it contacts the ground on the side, which lowers their profile. Again, some with extremely good flexibility will sit on that sideways foot to increase stability and decrease their height.

I've done all of that at one time or another, depending on the demands of both the terrain and the target. If you have the flexibility, it's useful to practice the different foot orientations in case you need them. I've found the major limitation to how long I can stay in this position is my foot going to sleep!

## Sitting

Of the shooting positions applicable to the fast-response nature of perimeter defense, sitting is — depending on individual physiology — in contention for the most stable. It therefore has great potential for precision.

On the other hand, the sitting position is the slowest to get into and out of, which is a detriment in defensive shooting. It also puts the shooter at the mercy of the ground; any debris or water will be keenly felt, which may rob the shooter of some precision potential.

The sitting position gives you very little to no ability to traverse (move sideways) to either follow a target or correct your alignment. Your position relative to the target is pretty well fixed. Thus, you'll need to make sure you're pointing at your target before you can actually shoulder your rifle. Only by practicing the sitting position will you know at what angle you need to sit in order to hold the rifle on target without muscle strain.

I consider the sitting position to be at the edge of plausibility for the task of perimeter defense. The time it takes to get into usually makes it unsuitable for anything but predator control at longer ranges.

There are many variants of the sitting position to accommodate the particular build of the shooter. They can roughly be divided into "knees up" and "knees down."

### Getting to the ground

Before you try any variation of the sitting position, it's important to note that just about everyone needs to use a hand to help get to the ground in a controlled and safe manner, and to get up again. This means at some point, you're likely to need to handle your rifle with the other hand, keeping the muzzle pointed in a generally safe direction.

In classes, this proves to be an issue for a small number of students, and for them I prescribe laying the rifle on the ground first. This of course makes the sitting position even slower to acquire.

I won't go into detail telling you how to sit down, because it's something you've been doing your entire life. But with the addition of the firearm, you need to pay close attention to the direction of the muzzle. This may affect exactly how you get from standing to sitting, and I recommend practicing with a broom or stick to make any necessary adjustments before trying it with a real gun.

Some people find it easier and safer to first drop to a double kneeling position (both knees on the ground), then bring their derriere to the ground to end up sitting. From there, it's easy to adjust the legs to either knees up or down.

*Knees up*

The knees-up position is the one you're likely to see in old shooting magazines and textbooks; it's the sitting position most often illustrated in military pictures. I personally find it somewhat unstable and difficult to use, but not everyone has the same opinion. The knees-up variation is less dependent on joint flexibility than the knees-down version.

To get into the classic knees-up position, sit down and place both feet on the ground directly in front of you. Ideally your soles should be flat on the ground, but many people are completely successful digging just their heels into the soil. Your feet should be roughly shoulder-width apart.

Now lean forward and place your elbows in front of your knees, so that your kneecap contacts the back of your upper arm above the elbow joint. Just as with the kneeling and squatting positions, avoid placing the elbow joint on the kneecap (bone-to-bone contact).

I find it difficult to keep my knees from moving sideways, like a tree in the wind, in this position. As a result, the knees-up variant isn't terribly stable for me. But many other shooters use it successfully.

*Knees down*

The knees-down variant is nothing more than a type of cross-legged sitting position, commonly used in meditation. Once you're sitting down, cross your legs at or just above the ankles and tuck them tightly into your body. The outside of your lower legs (the calf muscles) will actually be resting on the side and heel of your feet.

When you place any amount of pressure on your knees, it creates a tension that works like the aptly named scissors truss in architecture. The result is a very stiff and therefore stable platform.

All that's left to do is shoulder your rifle and lean forward to bring your elbows to the fleshy area on the sides of your knees. This puts you into a very "tucked in" position, which adds to the stability.

You can vary the height of your knees by choosing which ankle is in front of the other. For me, having the left ankle over the right one usually puts my knees in exactly the right position. Reversing the order drops my left knee, and since I'm a right-handed shooter, my support arm ends up lower and therefore the muzzle of my rifle points downward (which will be useful if I ever find myself shooting downhill). You'll need to experiment to find which position works well for you.

If you're extremely flexible, you may be able to get into and out of the knees-up position directly from standing, without an intermediate kneel or use of one hand for stabilization. There was a time in the not-too-distant past when I could do that, but with age has come a certain lack of flexibility that prevents me from doing so now. If you're young and limber, you might try it — with the caveat that you pay strict attention to the direction of your muzzle.

I know people who can start in a standing position, rifle shouldered and aimed at the target, and simply drop into the cross-legged sitting position — then stand up again, with the rifle never leaving their shoulder or deviating from their target. I don't think it has much utility for defense, but if nothing else, it impresses other shooters on the range!

## Prone

I don't teach the prone position in my perimeter defense classes, for a number of reasons.

First, while it's the most stable possible shooting position for most people, it's very slow to get into and out of and has very limited mobility — two characteristics that are antagonistic to the job of defensive shooting.

Prone is also only usable in a very narrow range of circumstances. The ground between you and your target must be flat (or slope downward noticeably), and there can't be any intervening obstacles. If you can't shoot under an obstacle, prone won't work.

Fences are the bane of the prone position, and tall grass may obstruct a clear view of your threat (particularly if the threat is of the four-legged variety). The prone position is also the least amenable to traverse to follow a target.

Finally, the prone position's precision potential relative to the job of perimeter defense is easily achieved by the other shooting positions, which aren't as limited in scope. In other words, the other shooting positions give nearly the same precision potential (well within the job required for perimeter defense) but are usable over a wider range of circumstances and conditions.

### *Be realistic*

If you look at your property and the places from which you're likely to need to shoot, I'll bet you won't find the kind of flat and unobstructed view needed for successfully using the prone position. There's almost no place on my property where it would be useful, and the overwhelming majority of my students have reported the same thing.

If I were to spend my time teaching the prone position, it would require me to take time away from other more important and useful skill development. If you were to spend your limited resources practicing it, you'd be neglecting the more widely useful shooting positions — especially the standing position, where almost everyone needs more practice.

In the final analysis, I suggest you direct the training resources you'd use practicing the prone position into getting better at shooting on your feet. That's your highest-probability shooting position, and you can always get better at it.

Leave the prone position for where it's most useful: on a nice, flat, smooth target range.

## Chapter Seventeen
# MOVING TO THE THREAT

As I've noted many times, the perimeter defense rifle is the defensive arm you must retrieve and take to the point where it can be employed. This is in distinct contrast to using the rifle to defend yourself inside your home, where the staging and employment points may be (and often are) in the same room.

The movement from the staging place to the point of use makes unique demands on how and what you train. How do you efficiently and safely get from where the rifle is stored to where it will be used?

### It starts with staging

In the last chapter on retrieval, you learned that how you store the gun — what it's in, how it's oriented, what else is around it, and so on — has an impact on how efficiently you can remove the rifle from its storage space and get it into action.

Retrieval revolves around the control point of the rifle. The control point is where the shooting hand grasps the gun, where you can easily access most of the controls and maintain orientation of the muzzle.

For an AR-15, the control point is the pistol grip. For a conventional rifle, it's the neck of the stock just behind the trigger.

Getting your shooting hand to the control point gives you the ability to move the rifle safely while still leaving you able to quickly ready the gun for shooting when necessary. Once your shooting hand is at the control point, your support hand can come on and off the rifle as necessary for you to navigate in your environment.

The worst combination is to have your support hand on the control point when you start moving. In order to use the rifle, your support hand has to be replaced with your shooting hand, then the support hand needs to move to the forearm or foregrip in order to shoot efficiently. This takes time and is prone to fumbling and mishandling.

For these reasons, it's best to start with your shooting hand on the control point. Arrange your storage or staging area to allow you to do so quickly and consistently.

## Hardware choices affect movement

Some rifles are easier to move with than others, especially when you're in a hurry.

There's no getting around the fact that the longer the barrel, the more cumbersome it is to maneuver quickly. This is true for both shooting and carrying. If you can afford a dedicated defensive rifle, you'll find the shorter barrels much easier to handle and transport.

It's surprising what a difference just a few inches of barrel makes in handling a rifle: A 16-inch barrel seems like a sports car compared to the stodgy sedan of the 20-inch barrel. And rifles with longer barrels (in the 22-inch and up range) are more like semi-trucks!

### *The bullpup advantage*

I mentioned the bullpup rifle in an earlier chapter. When moving, their ultra-compact design really shines. Getting the rifle out of its staging place, getting it into a position where it can be carried, maneuvering and running are all easier to do with the bullpup design.

It might surprise you to hear that I scoffed at their utility when first presented with the opportunity to use one, but I admit the handling qualities won me over. Training and practicing with the bullpup made me a fan. I'd never buy one for competitive target shooting, but as a defensive tool, they have a lot to offer.

Comparing a bullpup to even a compact AR-15 shows a stark difference. Equipped with the same 16-inch barrel, a .223/5.56 bullpup is significantly shorter than an already compact AR-15 carbine; seven inches shorter, in fact, in the case of a Steyr AUG bullpup compared to a Colt M4 Carbine.

But that's not the whole story. Both in my own use and with my students, I've observed that the most important dimension isn't overall length — rather, it's the distance from the control point to the muzzle. This distance directly affects how easily the gun is stabilized while moving rapidly and is a good predictor of the difficulty in keeping the muzzle under control.

Again using the same rifles for comparison, the bullpup has a nine-inch advantage over the AR-15. That's the same as the difference between a 16-inch and a 25-inch barrel, which is huge. No wonder the bullpup rifle handles better!

I'm not trying to convince you to rush out and buy a bullpup rifle. They come with a high price tag and some handling idiosyncrasies that you have to train and practice to overcome. These downsides shouldn't be ignored.

But at the same time, they do have significant and undeniable handling advantages in confined areas and during rapid movement. These likewise shouldn't be ignored.

*Magazine length*

Probably the most common perimeter defense rifle today is the ubiquitous AR-15 family, and by far the most popular magazine for this rifle has a 30-round capacity. Completely loaded, the 30-round magazine is heavy and protrudes from the rifle a good amount.

Because the AR-pattern rifle places the magazine in front of the control point, it affects the balance of the rifle to a significant degree. It's also in a position to more readily snag or catch on clothing, slings (another reason not to have one on your rifle), and other things in the environment.

Many years ago, I discovered the joys of the 20-round magazine for the AR-15. The 20-rounder is the original magazine capacity for the AR, and the one around which it was designed. The 30-round magazine came later in response to a need for higher capacity in fully automatic fire. The 30-round magazine became the military standard and naturally became the civilian standard as well.

The compact 20-round magazine hasn't lost its charms, however. It's lighter and much shorter, so it doesn't affect the rifle's balance to the degree that its larger brother does. Because it doesn't stick out from the rifle so far, it's also less likely to cause handling issues or snag on things. I like the 20-round magazine so much that it's become my standard for the AR-15.

Now I know some of you are thinking, "I want all the ammunition I can get in my rifle." This is a natural reaction: Everything in the gun press tells us that more is better, and many shooting classes are based on the notion that higher capacity is an absolute necessity. If someone subscribes to this point of view, I respectively submit that they haven't studied the defensive problem thoroughly.

You choose the rifle for perimeter defense because of its ability to project significant power, much greater than that of the handgun, at distance. As long as you actually hit your target in a vital zone, your fight is likely to be over with the first shot — in extreme cases, perhaps the second. Rifle fights just don't consume large amounts of ammunition, except in the movies.

It's quite rare (impossible, actually) to find a case where even a low-capacity rifle has been a disadvantage in a private-sector defensive encounter. Given that set of realities, even the "little" 20-round magazine will certainly be more than sufficient for any plausible incident you'll ever face. I don't consider a 20-rounder a handicap in any manner, shape or form*.

## Muzzle direction

This topic generates no end of discussion among defensive shooting instructors. Many of them argue quite vehemently that pointing the muzzle at the sky is never a safe direction and should therefore never be done. The problem with absolutes like this is they sometimes fail to take into account other safety considerations.

As a result, they usually recommend moving with the muzzle pointing down (sometimes referred to as "depressed"). The idea behind this is it's usually a safe direction and is consistent with the way most people teach to get the rifle into a shooting position.

But I've noticed that the muzzle-down position is difficult to run with. The weight distribution of most rifles leads to a pendulum effect, where the rifle's forward weight bias causes the muzzle to swing vigorously and requires two hands to stabilize. Moving around obstacles or in tight spaces often leads to the muzzle pointing at the shooter's feet — or the legs and feet of others in the environment.

The advantage is that, for many people, the muzzle is pointed in a generally safe direction: the ground. Of course, this isn't true for those whose guns are stored anywhere other than ground level. It's also not true if stairs need to be negotiated.

Remember that you're likely to need to move to the threat, which may be outside your house, and this may entail moving through multiple spaces and doorways in your home, and probably around objects or people. Your rifle needs to be oriented in such a way that you can move safely and quickly.

*Muzzle up to move quickly*

As a solution, I prescribe moving with the muzzle pointed straight up. By pointing the rifle up and curling your shooting arm into your torso, you effectively stabilize the rifle. The gun doesn't have the pendulum tendencies that come from having the muzzle pointed at the ground, and the risk of "flagging" your feet with the muzzle is eliminated. It also significantly reduces the chance that you'll accidentally point the muzzle at anyone else in the vicinity.

Because the muzzle is parallel to and within your body's outline, you considerably reduce the possibility of snagging or catching the muzzle, sights, or magazine on items in the environment. Finally, if you need to move very rapidly, such as running, the muzzle-up position lends itself to that more readily than just about any other position.

*Exceptions to muzzle-up carry*

I've found two exceptions to the muzzle-up position. First, if you're a tall person with a long-barreled rifle, your muzzle could hit the tops of doorframes as you move through them. I'm not that tall, and none of my perimeter defense rifles have exceptionally long barrels, so that hasn't been a problem for me. I haven't seen it in my students, either, but I offer it up as a possibility that you might consider if those variables apply to you.

Second, muzzle-up orientation may not be the best choice if your rifle is stored on the ground floor and bedrooms are above either the staging area or the path you'll take to reach the outside. The muzzle would necessarily be pointed at other people as you retrieve and move with your rifle, which is of course a safety issue.

In those cases, muzzle-down carry position may be preferable, if a bit less efficient.

**Running with the rifle**

Once you're clear of structures, you may find it necessary to really run with your rifle. This has happened to me on several occasions when I've become aware of a threat (every one of them was a predatory animal attacking livestock). I had to retrieve my rifle and run to a position where I had a clear shot at the attacker.

If you have a rifle with a pistol grip, such as an AR-15, it's very easy to run with the muzzle pointing straight up. You'll need to strongly clamp the rifle to your body with your bicep, but the advantage is that your support arm is free to swing normally to stabilize you while your feet are moving. This works particularly well for bullpup rifles, such as the Steyr AUG, and for rifles with thick buttstocks.

Conventionally stocked rifles are a little less amenable to this running position. I'm not saying it can't be done, only that there's less control than with pistol-gripped rifles. The distance between the point of control and the end of the butt tends to be shorter than that of pistol-gripped rifles, and as a result there's nothing for the bicep to clamp to your torso.

For these rifles, I suggest a method you've probably seen in war movies: port arms carry. This position keeps both hands on the rifle for maximum control and allows very rapid movement. In port arms, the rifle is carried on a diagonal across your body, muzzle up, with the shooting hand on the control point and the support hand on the forearm.

The exact angle of carry depends on many factors, including your own physiology, but should always be as close to vertical as possible for safety. In port arms you can run quite quickly and, on reaching the point where you need to stop and shoot, easily transition into a shooting position.

The position I've found least suited to running with the rifle is with the muzzle depressed, or pointed at the ground. If the shooting arm is held in a comfortable position for running, the support hand is uncomfortably extended and has reduced control over the muzzle. If the gun is brought up higher on the torso so the support hand is closer to the body and has better control, the shooting hand is put into a "chicken wing" position, which makes it difficult and uncomfortable to run.

Again, some will argue that moving with the muzzle pointed up is somehow unsafe. I submit that any time you move with the rifle and don't have full control over the swinging of the muzzle, *that* is unsafe — and I've found that trying to move with the muzzle pointed at the ground does not give the level of control necessary for safe gun handling.

**Pay attention to your trigger finger!**

Critical to safely and rapidly moving with a rifle is controlling your trigger finger. Even those with extensive training have a tendency to move their finger into the trigger guard when they start running.

If the trigger finger strays into the trigger guard while you're running, the chances of an unintentional shot go up dramatically. While carrying the gun cruiser-ready helps reduce the likelihood of that happening, and habitually keeping the safety on** adds another layer of accident prevention, your trigger finger discipline is the most important factor.

Some guns admittedly make this harder than others. The most popular bullpup rifles on the market, for example, don't have a trigger guard but rather a fence around the whole grip (they remind me of the guard on swords from the Civil War). This makes it much easier for the trigger finger to unintentionally stray onto the trigger while moving vigorously.

The best thing you can do is adopt a spot on the rifle, outside the trigger area, where your finger can safely rest when it's not needed to shoot. If there is a tactile feature you can feel to know your finger is correctly positioned, so much the better. Some shooters go to the trouble of adding such a feature (perhaps with a dab of glue) to which their finger can return. This tactile reminder serves as a touchpoint and makes it easier to imprint the safe position on your neural pathways.

*The competitive advantage*

This is one area where some experience in competitive action shooting (USPSA, IDPA, Three-Gun) is beneficial. Those games all require you to move rapidly with a loaded firearm, often multiple times during any one scenario (shooting stage). While the muzzle direction they mandate is artificial and may not always be applicable in a real-world environment, the trigger-finger discipline they rigidly enforce is extremely valuable and useful everywhere. In fact, I think their trigger-finger discipline may be the best part of the shooting games.

*Special: AR-15 issues*

I must add a caution for AR-15 users: Many people use the magazine release as their trigger finger "home position," which is understandable because it's placed at just the right spot for most people to touch with their finger (and was, I'm told, the reason it was placed there — it was easy to reach!). The problem is that it's quite easy to push inadvertently under even minor stress. I've seen students accidentally drop their magazines in class when they've encountered even a little stress in shooting an unfamiliar exercise.

I recommend finding another place for your trigger finger. If you have sufficiently long fingers and good flexibility, touching the shell deflector may be an option. Many people find the space above the magazine release comfortable, though the tactile sensation changes significantly if the dustcover is open or closed.

Some people place their trigger finger below the magazine release, touching the fence around that button with the side of their finger and gaining the desirable tactile reminder. I find this to be the least safe position, as the finger can easily snap onto the trigger accidentally if startled (or if you stumble while running). It also doesn't work with certain older or "retro" models which have no fence around the release button.

If your perimeter defense rifle is an AR-15, you'll need to experiment and find your best position that isn't on top of that magazine release.

*Special: Steyr AUG issues*

A few years ago, Steyr Arms arranged for the long-term loan of one of their AUG bullpup rifles so I could evaluate it for the role of home and perimeter defense, and to develop doctrine for its use in those contexts.

One issue I encountered immediately was with the safety. It's known as a cross-bolt safety, meaning it slides perpendicular to the rifle (i.e., left and right). This is similar to how most shotguns and many .22 rifles work.

The problem with the Steyr implementation is that the stock where the safety is located is radically angled down (toward the trigger) and inward. It's also completely smooth. The result is there's really no place to perch the trigger finger. Those with very long fingers and exceptional flexibility can reach up and touch the accessory rail on the top side of the receiver, but I can't — and neither could most of the people to whom I handed the rifle.

So the trigger finger can only sit alongside the stock, on that strong downward slope. Since, like most bullpups, the Steyr has no conventional trigger guard, it's absurdly easy for the finger to end up on the trigger even if the shooter is consciously trying not to touch it.

The protruding safety provides the only break in that smooth surface and is the likely place for the trigger finger to rest. Unfortunately, the safety is easily disengaged by the trigger finger and the shooter is back to the problem of the trigger finger sliding down to a trigger that is now off safe.

But I found a simple solution: Just curl the trigger finger around the safety. This provides a fence for the safety to guard against accidental deactivation, keeps the finger away from the trigger entirely, and gives the finger a nice resting position.

While I'd like to see Steyr add a small shelf for the trigger finger to the injection-molded stock, this turns out to be an acceptable workaround.

---

\* - ***Do not misconstrue my arguments as being in any way in favor of government-imposed magazine capacity restrictions***. *Just because I don't find 30-round (or larger) magazines terribly useful for the job of perimeter defense doesn't mean I think you shouldn't own them! Quite the contrary: I believe you, as a responsible gun owner, not some pandering politician, should be able to choose for yourself how many rounds your gun can carry. And after all, even my favored 20-round magazine is more than prohibitionists want us to have.*

\*\* - *Again, some guns (like the AR-15) cannot be put on safe if the hammer is not cocked, which is usually the case with an empty chamber.*

*Chapter Eighteen*

# SHOULDERING AND FIRING

When you get your rifle to the point where it can be employed against the threat, and you've made the decision to shoot, the mechanics of shooting come into play.

Over the years I've taken many rifle courses, most of them centering on "close-quarters battle" (CQB) and ostensibly self-defense, and all of them focused on the idea that the rifle was already on your shoulder (or positioned carefully just off the shoulder) when you decided to fire.

A typical shooting drill had students standing with the butt of the rifle touching the shoulder and the muzzle pointed sharply at the ground. On the signal, the rifles would be rotated or "hinged" upward and into a firing position. This type of drill assumed that the rifle was always on a sling, in both hands, and in a ready position.

As I mentioned at the outset, that's not been my experience in actual incidents. I've used a rifle many times on the homestead to protect against marauding predatory animals, and once against a human attacker*, and in no case was I set up and ready to shoot. In all cases I had to run to get my rifle, run back into the incident, and then make a decision to shoulder and fire (or not).

As you approach the scene, the point where you'll be able to employ the rifle, you'll likely be moving as quickly as conditions allow. As you do so, you'll be gathering information and using that to make a decision about your course of action: Do you need to shoot, or has the incident changed in such a way that shooting is not immediately necessary? Perhaps your own perception has changed or perhaps the attacker has changed his course of action; the latter happened to me when I was attacked. The attacker may have even left the scene before you could retrieve a rifle — as a bobcat did with my chickens (many times).

On the other hand, it may be clear that you need to incapacitate the attacker as quickly as possible, and you're moving into a position where you can do so cleanly and safely. You'll need to quickly transition between movement to the target and into a shooting position. That involves getting the rifle to your shoulder and firing.

**From moving to shooting**

The shouldering and firing process is often ignored by modern rifle instructors, yet it's the sequence you're most likely to need to know how to do.

The transport position — how you've held the rifle to enable the most rapid and efficient movement — is likely to be very different from your shooting position. You have to transition from that orientation to a shooting position, and do so very quickly. There isn't usually time for the contrived intermediate step of bringing the rifle to a low ready, positioning the butt of the rifle in just the right position on the shoulder, then swinging the rifle up to fire.

As I mentioned earlier, in the old days this process was called "snap shooting" — firing an accurate shot just as the gun is aligned on target and the butt touches the shoulder — and it has a lot of application in the context of perimeter defense.

The actual process varies a bit depending on just how you're carrying the rifle when you make the decision to shoot, but in general the rifle is brought to a horizontal position at roughly eye level, the butt pulled into the shoulder, and the shot fired.

Here's a more detailed look at the process.

1) As you reach the shooting point, you need to stop moving. Unless you're an extremely practiced "run-n-gun" competition shooter, it's quite difficult to shoot accurately while moving.

2) Based on your training and practice, decide from what position you'll need to shoot. The time pressure may deceive you into shooting from standing, even if that's not ideal for the shot you need to make. Let your experience and skill decide what your shooting position needs to be, and resolve to get into the position that will give you the best chance of an accurate shot into the area of precision the target is dictating.

Remember to keep your trigger finger in a safe position outside of the trigger guard until you actually need to fire.

3) Once in your shooting position, bring the rifle roughly horizontal and pointed at the target. This will likely require you to initially push the gun away from your body to clear any loose clothing as it comes into that horizontal position. If the gun started in a high muzzle position, the muzzle is brought down to align on target and the butt of the gun brought up. If starting from a muzzle-down position, the muzzle is brought up while the butt remains roughly stationary.

4) Bring the entire rifle into your line of sight to the target. In practice, I use my cheek as a reference point: When the stock touches my cheek, I know I have a good coarse alignment on target and the rifle is in the right position for me to transition my eyes to the sights**.

5) Once the gun is coarsely aligned on target, pull the gun back toward the shoulder. Two things happen during this movement: First, the sights are brought into play to more precisely align the gun on the target, and second, the safety is moved to the fire position while the finger remains safely off the trigger and, if possible, outside the trigger guard.***

6) As the butt of the rifle touches your shoulder, quickly confirm your sight alignment and aiming point, move your finger to the trigger so it touches the face of the trigger, and when ready, depress the trigger to fire the shot.

*The rifle is being moved from the muzzle-up transport position...*

*...and leveled at the target...*

*...and finally pulled back to contact the shoulder and fire the shot.*

This makes it sound a lot more complicated than it really is. As you practice, endeavor to make it a continuous, flowing movement. As you build familiarity, you'll discover it can be done very rapidly.

---

\* - *Because so many in the defensive training business trade on their experience shooting other people, even if it's only implied, I do not want this to be misconstrued: In my one incident against another human being, I fired no rounds and the encounter ended with no one hurt, which is the ideal outcome. I could have claimed complete justification in firing, and in fact came as close to doing so as having the rifle on my shoulder, aimed, with a round chambered and the safety off, before the encounter ended. I can therefore claim no special gunfighter status, and I sincerely hope that never changes.*

\*\* - *While this is not a book about close-quarters battle (CQB), or using the rifle inside of traditional handgun distances, if you are facing a very close target, you* *probably won't need to transition to your sights — the coarse alignment is often more than sufficient to achieve accurate shots.*

\*\*\* - *Some rifles, such as the M1 Garand, M1A, and Ruger Mini-14, have safeties inside the trigger guard and require the trigger finger to be inserted into the guard to operate. This is not an ideal arrangement, and if you have such a rifle, you must be extremely diligent to keep the trigger finger off the trigger until you've decided to actually fire a round.*

*Chapter Nineteen*

# TRAINING AND PRACTICING PERIMETER DEFENSE

Few courses teach the mechanics applicable to perimeter defense.* The training market today is focused on either target shooting or "close-quarters battle," neither of which is really what you need.

Most people live in urban or suburban areas, where the kind of defense we've been discussing isn't part of their reality, so the lack of suitable classes is understandable. But if you need those skills, that isn't much of a consolation!

## Alternative classes

If you can't find (or can't travel to) a class, I suggest looking for a traditional basic rifle class. What you want to see is instruction in the basic rifle shooting stances and the chance to refine your shooting in each. You probably won't be exposed to the rapid shooting, particularly the snap shooting, necessary for efficient defensive use, but you'll at least get some good solid fundamentals.

Once you have those fundamentals, you can practice on your own. But first, you need to find a range. That's actually harder than it sounds!

## Picking a shooting range

Rifle ranges are typically set up for target shooting. They have benches at which patrons are supposed to sit and rest their rifles, and often there are enforced rules about "rapid fire" — usually defined as shooting more than one round per second. It's also not uncommon for restrictions to be made on the kind of targets allowed: Silhouettes with vaguely human contours may not be permitted, and all targets must be placed at a common fixed distance from the shooters.

These arrangements don't lend themselves to practicing realistically for perimeter defense, for which you need several things in a range:

- Targets that approximate the size and vital zones of the threats you're likely to encounter in your environment
- Flexibility to place those targets at any plausible distance, including random distances from the shooter
- Freedom to shoot from the relevant "field" positions (standing, squatting, kneeling, and sitting)
- Ability to start in a transport/moving orientation and get rapidly into a firing stance (snap shooting)
- Ideally, the chance to practice the full suite of perimeter defense skills: run to a stored rifle, retrieve the rifle, then move with the gun to a point where you can fire at a realistic target at a plausible (and not exact) distance as rapidly as you deem necessary.

While you might find a range that will allow you to achieve the first four points, it's rare indeed to find a range that will allow the fifth (and most realistic) one. If you have such a range, consider yourself lucky!

### Where to look

That isn't to say such ranges don't exist. If your area has a range that hosts 3-Gun competitions, it probably has an appropriate range (usually a large bay with berms on three sides). You may need to take a class or pass a qualifying test to prove you're skilled enough to be trusted on what amounts to a free or unsupervised range, but the benefits to your skill development are worth the bureaucratic hassle.

Some informal ranges on public lands (state forests and even some federal lands) are also suitable for this kind of realistic practice.

Finally, to practice realistically, you must commit to doing so. It's easy to decide you don't want to drive all the way to the range that allows you to practice your skills and instead accept the limitations at the closest facility. Many people rationalize this by saying, "Some trigger time is better than none."

I hate to be blunt, but that's a cop-out. Just pulling a trigger isn't going to prepare you for the whole task of defending yourself, your loved ones, or your homestead from an attacker. The shooting part is almost the easiest; it's the rest of it that's hard.

Getting to the gun and bringing the gun to the shooting point, then being able to recognize how much skill you need to apply in what time frame to land accurate shots on any target — all while being out of breath — is the job at hand, and isolating just one part (the trigger pulling) isn't helpful to the rest of it.

If you're serious about developing your ability to defend yourself at distance with a rifle, you need the whole package. It's worth a little effort (and a longer drive) to do so.

**What to practice**

Think in terms of the sequence of events you might go through in a real incident:

- Recognizing that you need your rifle for the attack that's unfolding
- Getting to where the rifle is stored or staged
- Retrieving the rifle

- Moving quickly with the rifle to the point where it will be used
- Putting the rifle into a ready condition (chambering a round)
- Deciding what shooting position (stance) is appropriate
- Quickly getting into that position
- Aligning (aiming) the rifle on the target
- Quickly making an accurate shot
- Reloading or readying the rifle for another shot if necessary

Recreate those steps as closely as you can in your practice environment. You might not be able to do every one every time, but sequencing is important. For example, if you're at a range that doesn't allow you to stage your rifle and move with it to simulate retrieval and running to the point of employment, you might at least be able to start with the rifle in cruiser ready and practice chambering a round and quickly putting an accurate shot on the target. Unload, put the rifle back into cruiser ready, and do it again.

Most of your practice should be from the standing position, focusing on the snap shot, because that's the most plausible defensive shooting position. Perhaps 20% of your practice should be from the other shooting positions.

Use different targets, at different heights from the ground if possible, to simulate both animal and human threats. Shoot at different distances, out to the limits of your property line or about 100 to 150 yards.

Remember the overriding purpose of your practice is to enable you to make a quick and accurate first shot at any plausible distance, on any plausible target, from an appropriate shooting position. If you keep that in mind, you won't go too far wrong.

---

\* - *With all due modesty, may I suggest my own Perimeter Defense rifle course?*

*http://www.grantcunningham.com/self-defense-training/perimeter-defense-rifle/*

*If I'm not teaching in your area, perhaps you can host me at your local shooting range. I travel all over the United States to teach, and I'd be happy to discuss coming to your town. Email me at info@grantcunningham.com for more information.*

*Chapter Twenty*
# PARTING THOUGHTS

I hope this book has opened your eyes to both the myths and the realities of using the rifle as a defensive tool. The rifle has enormous capabilities, requires a certain skill level to use effectively, and always carries with it immense responsibility.

Whenever you use your rifle to protect yourself and your loved ones, or to protect your homestead from predators, you must do so lawfully and ethically. If you need to kill a predatory animal, do so quickly and minimize the animal's suffering.

If you face a human attacker, ask yourself if you need to pull the trigger. Is that person posing an immediate threat to your life or the life of another innocent? If he's merely stealing property, that isn't an appropriate use of force (no matter what the law might "allow" in your state). The lawfully wielded firearm is an instrument of lethal capability and should only be used to prevent the death of another.

Always remember: Just because you can, doesn't mean you should. Balance your skill with compassion and an understanding of the ethics of self-defense, and you'll be in the very best position to keep yourself, your family, and your homestead safe.

# GET YOUR FREE AMMUNITION BOOK!

I've written a book on choosing defensive ammunition that will help you pick the right ammo for your handgun, rifle, or shotgun. It explains how ammunition works in simple terms and what you should look for at your local gun store.

You can get your FREE copy of *How To Choose Self Defense Ammunition* just by clicking or going to this link on my site:
www.getgrant.us/PYH

# FACEBOOK DISCUSSION GROUP

If you have a Facebook account, please join me and the other readers of *Protecting Your Homestead* in our own private Facebook group!

The Protecting Your Homestead Facebook group is a place for you to discuss all of the important topics in this book. You can ask questions, get answers, network with other preparedness-minded people, and get the motivation you need to stay on the path to balance and peace.

It's a private group, so outsiders can't see what's posted there. Your discussions will only be visible to other like-minded members!

Here's the link to our group page. Just click on "Join" and you'll be added to the group:

https://www.facebook.com/groups/protectingyourhomestead/

## ALSO BY GRANT CUNNINGHAM

Prepping For Life: The balanced approach to personal security and family safety

Protect Yourself With Your Snubnose Revolver

How To Choose Defensive Ammunition

Handgun Training - Practice Drills For Defensive Shooting

Defensive Revolver Fundamentals

Defensive Pistol Fundamentals

The 12 Essentials of Concealed Carry

Gun Digest Book Of The Revolver

Shooter's Guide To Handguns

Click or visit www.grantcunningham.com

for more information or to purchase!

# ABOUT THE AUTHOR

I've been studying the field of self defense and personal preparedness since the early 1990s. I've attended hundreds of hours of training in many related fields, from defensive firearms to immediate trauma care to how predatory criminals think, all aimed at learning what's valuable and what's not. I even did the coursework for a degree in Emergency Management, just to find out how professionals plan for a wide range of potential hazards!

What I learned from my education is that there's no "one size fits all" solution to personal security, and that glib answers don't keep people safer. I've taken this insight and applied it to everything I teach. The result is the information that I've put into my many books (nine so far!), workshops and classes.

The basics of self sufficiency were a large part of my growing up on a small farm in rural Oregon during the turbulence of the 1960s and 1970s. My childhood was filled with typical rural activities such as hunting and fishing, and guns were a natural part of that ecosystem. On a farm the firearm is a tool, just like any other tool, and they represented work. I learned they have a proper use and a misuse. As a consequence I neither feared nor fetishized them.

I believe in the civil rights of all Americans, including the right to defend oneself using the most efficient means possible. I also believe that with rights always come responsibilities, and that we often talk far too much about the former and not nearly enough about the latter. I remain a strong believer in the value of our country's Constitution — even if our application of that document is sometimes flawed.

I want to help you by finding the best information from the most reliable sources and distilling it into relevant, actionable lessons that you can put to use in your life. In my books and workshops I focus on teaching the most important skills, and doing so in a way that leads you to competency and long-term retention. Whether self defense, situational awareness, or disaster preparedness, I always focus on you, your life, and your needs.

Today I put everything I've learned to use on my own small farm in the mountains of rural Oregon, where I live with my wife and far too many cats.

**Protecting Your Homestead:**

*Using a rifle to defend life on your property*

By Grant Cunningham

Published by Personal Security Institute LLC

Copyright 2018, Grant Cunningham and Personal Security Institute LLC.

All rights reserved.

*Except for brief passages for the purpose of review, no portion of this publication may be reproduced or transmitted in any form or by any means without permission in writing from the author.*

Click or visit:

www.grantcunningham.com

www.ingramcontent.com/pod-product-compliance
Lightning Source LLC
Chambersburg PA
CBHW071610080526
44588CB00010B/1087